D1707914

SPEECHCRAFT

DISCOURSE PRONUNCIATION FOR ADVANCED LEARNERS

Laura D. Hahn

Wayne B. Dickerson

MICHIGAN SERIES IN ENGLISH FOR
ACADEMIC & PROFESSIONAL PURPOSES

Ann Arbor
THE UNIVERSITY OF MICHIGAN PRESS

PREFACE

Speechcraft: Discourse Pronunciation for Advanced Learners is a pronunciation textbook primarily for advanced nonnative speakers of English who expect to interact with native speakers in academic and professional settings. It is designed to provide rules, strategies, and contextualized practice in the stress, rhythm, and melody of English words and discourse—those features of English pronunciation that affect intelligibility the most.

The *Speechcraft* materials consist of a core textbook, workbooks for specific audiences that expand on and contextualize the content of the core textbook, and accompanying audiotapes. The textbook and workbooks interrelate as follows.

Speechcraft

	Introductory Topics	
Textbook	Groundwork	
	Academic/Professional Terms	Workbooks
	Discourse Level Topics	
Textbook	Discourse Foundations	
	Discourse Domains	Workbooks
	Word Level Topics	
Textbook	Word Foundations	
Textbook (Patterns)	Word Stress Domains	Workbooks (Practice and Review)
	Construction Stress	Workbooks
	Supplementary Topics	
Textbook	Suggestions for Instructors	
Textbook	Vowel and Consonant Prediction Patterns	
(for units in Textbook)	Answers	(for units in Workbooks)
	Oral Practice Projects	Workbooks
	Checklist for Covert Rehearsal	Workbooks

Focus of *Speechcraft*

Speechcraft meets the needs of learners in four major ways.

- Its emphasis on stress, rhythm, and melody provides learners with information and practice on the aspects of pronunciation that are most relevant to their task of expressing meaning intelligibly.
- In addition to its systematic treatment of word level and phrase level topics, *Speechcraft* also handles extended discourse.
- It provides abundant and diverse practice exercises that reflect linguistic and cultural contexts appropriate to the learners' needs and allows them to use their own language meaningfully.
- *Speechcraft* puts learners in control of their own improvement by providing them with tools for self-monitoring and self-correction, namely, systematic rules about stress, rhythm, and melody and ample practice applying those rules to their own speech.

Core Textbook

The core text is organized as follows.

1. **Groundwork** introduces the basics that all students must become familiar with before proceeding with the rest of the text. These basics include an explanation of the purpose and scope of the materials, an overview of the sound system, and an overview of the concepts and conventions that the rest of the *Speechcraft* materials will use and expand on. The Groundwork section also serves to emphasize the interrelatedness of all components of the English pronunciation system.
2. **Discourse Level Topics** focus on the features that give English discourse its unique rhythm—features such as message units, rhythmic contrasts, natural speech phenomena, intonation, and (at an introductory level) the placement of primary stress.
3. **Word Level Topics** focus on the placement of major stress on polysyllabic words, e.g., *technícian, téchnical, technicálity.* These lessons show learners how to identify for themselves the syllable containing the major stress in thousands of academic and professional terms.
4. The **Appendixes** provide suggestions for instructors, vowel and consonant prediction patterns, and answers to the exercises.

Workbooks

A workbook is a required accompaniment to the core text, as the topics in the core text cannot be treated fully without the contextualized practice in the workbooks. The workbooks are organized as follows.

1. **Word Stress Domains: Primary Stress and Intonation.** These sections provide focused practice on several primary stress and intonation patterns that are important for academic and professional discourse. Communicative activities are included.
2. **Word Level Topics: Contextualized Practice and Review.** All word level work introduced in the core text is practiced in a larger discoursal context, where word rhythm makes a direct contribution to the larger rhythm of utterances. Communicative activities are included.
3. **Appendixes.** Answers to the exercises and supplementary practice material are included.

Audiotapes
Audiotapes of dialogs and other discourse in the core text and in the workbooks are available on audiotape for students' use in practice.

SPECIAL ACKNOWLEDGMENTS

The authors would like to acknowledge the role of Greta Muller Levis as a consultant for *Speechcraft.* Her feedback on and contributions to this project early in its development were invaluable to us. We thank her for sharing her ideas, helping us work out the materials—from conceptual framework to details of early lessons—and trying out the lessons in class.

In addition, Barbara Bair has provided us with a great deal of detailed feedback and suggestions for improvement. We are grateful for her thoughtful comments.

Finally, we wish to thank others too numerous to mention who have given us technical, instructional, and moral support throughout this project.

The concepts, stress rules, and terminology in *Speechcraft* are drawn with permission from *Stress in the Speech Stream: The Rhythm of Spoken English, Student Manual* by Wayne B. Dickerson (1989). Students and teachers who wish to explore the concepts in more detail should consult this valuable resource. *Stress in the Speech Stream* provides a more thorough treatment of the word and phrase stress rules, as well as useful spelling patterns for predicting the vowel and consonant sounds of English words. For more information about this textbook, you may contact the author at <dickrson@uiuc.edu> or at 7 Hale Haven Ct., Savoy, IL 61874.

CONTENTS

Contents

GROUNDWORK

Groundwork introduces basic information about English pronunciation and pronunciation learning. It contains an explanation of the purpose and scope of the materials, an overview of the sound system, and information on the concepts and conventions that the rest of the text will use. Therefore students should go through Groundwork before proceeding with the rest of *Speechcraft*.

The following lessons are covered in Groundwork.

G-1

PURPOSE AND SCOPE
OF *SPEECHCRAFT*

SELF-REFLECTION

☞ Answer these questions for yourself on a separate piece of paper. Be as complete and as specific as possible.

1. How would you describe your English pronunciation ability?
2. How would you describe the English pronunciation you would *like* to have?
3. How would you describe your fluency in English?
4. How would you describe the fluency you would *like* to have?
5. What do you think your strengths are in speaking English?
6. Why do you want to improve your pronunciation?
7. How much time per day do you spend talking with native speakers of English?

A DIALOG ABOUT PRONUNCIATION LEARNING

Why is pronunciation relevant to communication?

It is a challenge to be an effective communicator even in one's native language. It takes a great deal of skill to explain, motivate, define, summarize, etc., with clarity. And doing these things in a language and culture that are not your own is an even greater challenge. Therefore a solid grasp of the linguistic and cultural features of your academic or professional context is critical to your success.

For many nonnative speakers, one of the most salient of these features is pronunciation. Native speakers will be able to interact naturally with you only if they can recognize and comprehend the words and phrases you use. So control over the sound system of English is essential if you want to be intelligible to others.

I've studied English pronunciation before, but it hasn't helped. Why?

Many people think of an English pronunciation class as one where students' vowel and consonant sounds are corrected. Most pronunciation teachers and most of their students, however, have found such pronunciation work to be only minimally satisfying. They report that such in-class drill and correction have little effect in "real life."

Recent research and experience, however, have led us to revise our view of what English pronunciation is all about. Following are more up-to-date assumptions about pronunciation learning and teaching.

- English rhythm and melody, more than vowels and consonants, play a direct role in communicating meaning in spoken discourse.
- Pronunciation learning happens because of what students do, not what teachers do.
- Pronunciation improvement (and transfer to "real life") takes place gradually—requiring more time than a semester. It also takes place primarily in situations outside of class, that is, in intense, private practice called *covert rehearsal.*
- A valuable resource for effective covert rehearsal is a knowledge of the rules about the way English pronunciation works.

Because *Speechcraft* follows these assumptions, it is not a conventional pronunciation textbook.

So how does Speechcraft *work?*

The *Speechcraft* core text and workbooks provide the resources you need for you to improve your ability to

- produce natural English speech,
- perceive natural English speech, and
- predict the correct pronunciation of words and phrases.

These materials offer guidance, techniques, and practice opportunities for you to apply principles of English rhythm and melody to your own speech—specifically, the language of your academic or professional context. The practice opportunities in *Speechcraft* are identified by the hand symbol (☞).

If pronunciation improvement is my responsibility, what is my role?

There is a cycle of learning activities that will help you improve your pronunciation.

1. Preparation on your own

In *Speechcraft* you will learn how to analyze the words and phrases you are planning to use in your academic or professional setting and how to predict the sounds, rhythms, and melodies you will use. The purpose of the rules you will learn is not for use in real life conversation. That is an unrealistic expectation. Rather, the rules are to be used where real pronunciation learning takes place: in covert rehearsal. Covert rehearsal involves private oral practice—using your predictions to shape and reshape your delivery.

Preparation is primarily done outside of class. Your written homework will help you practice prediction and will provide the basis for your covert rehearsal. In order for you to do the homework well and master the materials, it is very important that you read everything in each assignment. That is, read all of the explanations and notes very carefully before you do the written work.

You will also notice that each written assignment includes instructions such as "Read each word (or dialog or passage) aloud." This is the most important instruction! The written work is simply not useful unless you practice it aloud and internalize the patterns you have analyzed so that you can produce them naturally.

In addition, *Speechcraft*'s audiotapes can guide your oral practice as well.

2. Oral work in class
In class, you will put your own preparation into use. You will have the opportunity to apply all of the rules and strategies for speaking that you have been working on. There will be a variety of speaking activities to check your preparation of the material at hand. This is an excellent chance for you to practice in a safe environment, so be sure to participate actively.

3. Feedback
You will receive feedback on your oral work, which includes your performance in class and the audiotapes you make. You can use this feedback to start the cycle again—in your prediction and covert rehearsal.

There is great value in getting involved in this cycle of pronunciation learning. That is, the cycle is useful far beyond this textbook or any class you are in. As you progress to your own speaking activities, you can continue to apply the strategies you learn. Whenever you prepare a lecture, a group discussion, or a seminar, you will be able to prepare the pronunciation of the words and phrases you will use. You can practice aloud and do exercises that focus on the required sounds, rhythms, and melodies. And you can monitor yourself or even solicit feedback—from your peers and others—to continue to improve.

What exactly is covert rehearsal, and how can I do it?

Covert rehearsal refers to the activity of private, focused practice that you do by yourself. This is how the majority of language learning takes place: by yourself, not in class. Good language learners practice by themselves and do it a lot. How?

- Spend time every day talking to yourself in English. When you are walking to and from classes, while you are doing your laundry, before you fall asleep at night, you should be talking to yourself in English. Think about the discussion you will lead the next day, imagine that you are in a seminar, and participate in made-up conversations with your co-workers.
- Make your practice effective. While you are thinking about the talking you may be doing, listen carefully to your articulations. Critique the accuracy and fluency of your language use. Examine your own speech to see if it follows the language rules you know. If it does, practice it again and again until it comes naturally! If it doesn't seem right, analyze what you do and make improvements.
- Practice in a variety of ways. Talk aloud to yourself (even if you feel strange!). Write an outline of a short talk and "talk" it aloud. You can also tape-record yourself and listen critically to what you said. Some students also benefit from talking in front of a mirror, so that they can observe their facial movements and expressions.

How long will it take for me to improve?

Realistically speaking, learning pronunciation skills takes time. Many factors, including your current level of ability, the amount of practice you do, and your own learning style, will affect the amount of progress you make. Of course, the more you practice, the more you will improve. But given the complexity of the sound system of English, it is unrealistic to expect 100 percent mastery of it in one semester or even longer. In fact, it is important to remember that pronunciation ability is not "all or nothing." It is the case that, for a given word or phrase pattern, progress may actually be in the form of being able to identify correct and incorrect versions, mastering the main stress, or even pronouncing something right 50 percent of the time instead of 10 percent of the time.

You need to think critically about what progress you think you can make and set some goals.

MORE REFLECTION

☞ Answer these questions for yourself on a separate piece of paper. Be as complete and as specific as possible.

1. Write three or four of your own sentences that summarize the points in "A Dialog about Pronunciation Learning."
2. Do you do covert rehearsal? If so, describe it and decide whether you can

improve your strategies. If you don't do covert rehearsal at all now, how can you get started?

3. What goals do you have for improving your pronunciation? Be as specific as possible.

SOUNDS: OVERVIEW OF CONSONANTS AND VOWELS

This section introduces the English consonant and vowel system. Although consonant and vowel work is not the focus of *Speechcraft*, it is important for you to learn these English sounds and the symbols that represent them. You will be practicing many of the most challenging sounds in class. And your instructor will be using these symbols to give you feedback throughout the course.

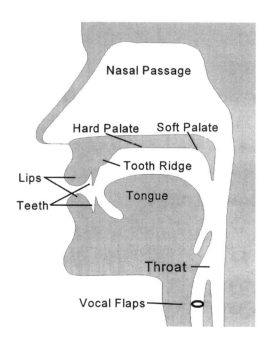

English Consonant Sounds

A I R F L O W		V O I C E	PLACES OF ARTICULATION						
			Two Lips	Lip and Teeth	Tongue and Teeth	Tongue and Tooth Ridge	Tongue and Hard Palate	Tongue and Soft Palate	Throat
S T O P S		Vl Vd	/p/ pack /b/ back			/t/ tie /d/ die	/tʃ/ choke /dʒ/ joke	/k/ key /g/ gold	
C O N T I N U A N T S	Continuant Type								
	Fricatives	Vl Vd		/f/ fine /v/ vine	/θ/ thank /ð/ than	/s/ sip /z/ zip	/ʃ/ she /ʒ/ vision		/h/ hot
	Nasals	Vd	/m/ meet			/n/ now		/ŋ/ ring	
	Liquids	Vd				/l/ last	/r/ red		
	Glides	Vd	/w/ walk				/y/ yet		

English Vowel Sounds

Tongue Position / Tongue Height	FRONT	CENTRAL	BACK
HIGH	/iy/ feed /ɪ/ fit	(i) cóuntr̲y (u) écr̲u̲	/uw/ boot /ʊ/ bush
MID	/ey/ fade /ɛ/ fed	/ɜr/ cúrler (ər) /ʌ/ cústom (ə)	/ow/ bone (o) bráv̲o̲
LOW	/æ/ fad	/ɑ/ cot	/ɔ/ boss
Complex Vowels /ay/ fine /ɔy/ coin /aw/ bound			

VOWEL QUALITY

English vowels can be classified into two basic groups: full vowels, which have major or minor stress, and reduced vowels, which are unstressed. Both full vowels and reduced vowels have glided and unglided forms.

	Glided	Unglided
Full Vowels (stressed)	/iy/, /ey/, /ay/, /ɔy/, /ow/, /uw/, /aw/, /ɜr/	/ɪ/, /ɛ/, /æ/, /ʌ/, /ɑ/, /ʊ/, /ɔ/
Reduced Vowels (unstressed)	(ər)	(ɪ, i, u, ə, o)

The vowels *(i, u, o)* are unstressed counterparts of /iy/, /uw/, /ow/, respectively. The vowel /ɪ/ can occur in both stressed and unstressed syllables.

NOTE: The vowel /uw/ is sometimes pronounced with /y/ before it, e.g., *mute* /myuwt/. See Appendix 2, section E, for patterns predicting the use of the /y/.

VOWEL AND CONSONANT SYMBOLS
PRACTICE

☞ a. Listen to your instructor read each set of words.
   b. For each word between slashes, circle the word whose spelling matches
      the sounds represented by the symbols.

Example:

/tawnz/	tones	tongs	(towns)
1. /rɑŋ/	rang	wrong	ran
2. /ʤɛlo/	yellow	jello	cello
3. /mæʧ/	match	mat	mash
4. /liyʒənd/	legioned	lesioned	legend
5. /pəliys/	police	policy	please
6. /kɔl/	call	coil	cowl
7. /pɜrt/	part	putt	pert
8. /lʊk/	Luke	look	luck
9. /lowd/	laud	loud	load
10. /rayvəl/	rival	ravel	revile

BEYOND SOUNDS: OVERVIEW OF THE WORD LEVEL

☞ Listen to this Model Dialog. Then practice it.

A: What's the matter?

B: I'm really in a rush.

A: Do you need any help?

B: Let's see . . . Maybe you can help me finish these graphs.

A: No problem. Are you always so busy?

B: Well, today I'm especially busy. This morning, I'm finishing a review of an article, and I'm chairing a staff meeting. Then I need to get ready to present a seminar.

A: What's the topic of the seminar?

B: You'll never believe it. It's "How to manage your time."

This Model Dialog contains examples of the basic rhythm and melody patterns introduced in Groundwork G-3 and G-4.

PATTERNS

Why study English words?

- Good English rhythm is essential for delivering a clear oral message to listeners. Words with more than one syllable—"polysyllabic" words—have their own rhythm.
- Academic and technical language frequently includes polysyllabic words. In many speaking situations, you often introduce or use specialized terminology. If you incorrectly pronounce a word that your listeners are unfamiliar with, they may not understand the term at all and miss an important part of your message as a result.
- Words contribute to the larger rhythm of utterances. You seldom pronounce one word by itself. Instead, you use many words together in one utterance. In order for the phrase to be clear, the words have to be clear. That is, good word rhythm leads to good phrase rhythm.
- Being able to perceive and produce good word rhythm will increase understanding. But how do you know what rhythm a word should have? By using a few simple rules, you will be able to predict the rhythm of thousands of academic or technical terms . . . and thus improve your own speech.

What will be covered in "Beyond Sounds: Overview of the Word Level"?

This section will introduce you to these important concepts.

Syllables
Word Rhythm: Alternations and Major Stress
Compound Constructions

SYLLABLES

Why are we going to study syllables?

- Syllables are basic to speech. We speak in syllables strung together.
- Syllables carry a beat. By changing the stress and vowels of syllables we create the alternations of English-style rhythm.
- Syllables contain clues to word stress. Information inside of syllables can help us predict the major stress of words—another part of English-style rhythm.
- Syllables can be troublesome to nonnative speakers, who frequently drop syllables from words when they should not be dropped. We will work on pronouncing such syllables correctly instead of dropping them.

So, specifically what is a syllable?

The polysyllabic words in the Model Dialog are *italicized.*

A: What's the *matter?*
B: I'm *really* in a rush.
A: Do you need *any* help?
B: Let's see . . . *Maybe* you can help me *finish* these graphs.
A: No *problem.* Are you *always* so *busy?*
B: Well, *today* I'm *especially busy.* This *morning,* I'm *finishing* a *review* of an *article,* and I'm *chairing* a staff *meeting.* Then I need to get *ready* to *present* a *seminar.*
A: What's the *topic* of the *seminar?*
B: You'll *never believe* it. It's "How to *manage* your time."

1. Syllables carry the beat, or the pulse, of a word.

One Syllable	Two Syllables	Three or More Syllables
what's	matter	appreciate
rush	finish	especially
help	problem	seminar

Other examples:

One Syllable	Two Syllables	Three or More Syllables
vent	invent	invention
port	support	unsupportive
form	formal	formality
state	instate	reinstated

2. The beat is carried primarily in the vowel sound of the syllable. Therefore, each syllable has one and only one vowel sound.

One vowel sound can be represented by one or more vowel letters.

One Vowel Sound, One Vowel Letter	One Vowel Sound, Two Vowel Letters	Two Vowel Sounds, Two Vowel Letters
th<u>a</u>t /æ/	y<u>ou</u> /uw/	apprec<u>ia</u>te /i/ + /ey/
v<u>e</u>st /ɛ/	n<u>ee</u>d /iy/	t<u>ui</u>tion /uw/ + /ɪ/
wh<u>i</u>ch /ɪ/	r<u>ea</u>ch /iy/	r<u>ei</u>nstated /iy/ + /ɪ/

☛ **EXERCISE 1.**   a. Read aloud the italicized words in the Model Dialog.
                       b. Then read the dialog again and notice the contribution of word rhythm to the rhythm of the whole dialog.

A: What's the *matter?*
B: I'm *really* in a rush.
A: Do you need *any* help?
B: Let's see . . . *Maybe* you can help me *finish* these graphs.
A: No *problem.* Are you *always* so *busy?*
B: Well, *today* I'm *especially busy.* This *morning,* I'm *finishing* a *review* of an *article,* and I'm *chairing* a staff *meeting.* Then I need to get *ready* to *present* a *seminar.*
A: What's the *topic* of the *seminar?*
B: You'll *never believe* it. It's "How to *manage* your time."

☛ **EXERCISE 2.**   Remember: Each syllable has one and only one vowel sound.
                       a. How many syllables are in each word?
                       b. Read the words and tap the syllables as you say them.

Example:
     intérpret   __3__

1. músic   _____   6. téchnical   _____

2. músical   _____   7. Chicágo   _____

3. musicólogist   _____   8. cámpus   _____

4. desk   _____   9. íncident   _____

5. technológical   _____   10. incidéntal   _____

ALTERNATIONS

> A polysyllabic word in English has two features:
> Alternations and Major Stress.

At the word level, syllables alternate between stressed and unstressed. Stressed syllables differ from unstressed syllables in three ways: vowel length, vowel quality, and pitch.

1. **Vowel Length.** The vowel of a stressed syllable is stretched out in duration. The vowel of an unstressed syllable is said more quickly. This is the most important contrast to the listener; this is the contrast that creates an English-style rhythm.

Stressed Syllables	Unstressed Syllables
stretched out	quick
i n for m **a** tion	i n for m a **tio**n
<----> <---->	>-< >-<

2. **Vowel Quality.** Stressed syllables have full vowel sounds. Unstressed syllables have one of the five reduced vowels.

Stressed Syllables	Unstressed Syllables
full vowels—	reduced vowels—
vowels other than /ə/, /i/, /ər/, /u/, /o/	/ə/, /i/, /ər/, /u/, /o/
i n f o r m **a** t i o n	i n f **o** r m a t i **o** n
/ɪ/ /ey/	/ər/ /ə/

NOTE: Pronouncing unstressed vowels.

Use /ə/ or /ər/

- when the vowel is followed by a consonant
  (but not an ending like *-s, -ing,* or *-ly*)   infŏrmátiŏn
- with a final *a*   cómmă

Use /i/, /u/, or /o/

- at the end of a word   stráteğy, mén̆u, dítt̄o
- before an ending   strategı̆es, mén̆us, díttŏing
- before another vowel sound   pronuncı̆átion, contín̆uous, céllŏist

3. **Pitch.** Stressed syllables are often higher in pitch than unstressed syllables. Unstressed syllables are usually lower in pitch than stressed syllables.

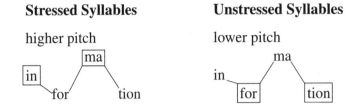

Stressed Syllables   **Unstressed Syllables**

higher pitch   lower pitch

The rhythmic alternation of length, vowel quality, and pitch from stressed to unstressed syllables is regular in most words. In some words, the alternation is not perfectly regular. For example, in "noninformational," "non" and "in" are two adjacent stressed syllables, and "tion" and "al" are two adjacent unstressed syllables.

Syllable Characteristics	Syllable Stress	
	Stressed Syllables	**Unstressed Syllables**
Vowel length Vowel quality Pitch	Stretched out syllables Full vowels Higher pitch	Quick syllables Reduced vowels Lower pitch

MAJOR STRESS

1. There are three levels of word stress: major stress, minor stress, and unstressed, each indicated with a different stress mark. Notice that we put the
   stress mark over the vowel.

major stress	(′)	informátion, artículated
minor stress	(`)	ìnformation, àrticulàted
unstressed	(˘)	infŏrmatiŏn, articŭlatĕd

2. Each word contains one and only one major stress. This syllable is more
   stretched out, has a full vowel, and has a higher pitch than all the other syllables. Depending on the word, there may be any number of minor stressed
   and unstressed syllables (see the examples above).
3. Word stress is predictable. *Speechcraft* will show you how to accurately put
   the major stress on thousands of polysyllabic English words, without looking them up in the dictionary.

Summary

Polysyllabic words have a rhythm created by alternations of stressed and unstressed syllables and by one major stress.

☞ **EXERCISE 3.**   Read each word aloud three times, focusing on the alternations and stress. Remember:
   Stressed syllables: stretched-out, full vowels on a
   higher pitch
   Unstressed syllables: quicker, reduced vowels on a
   lower pitch

ìnfŏrmátiŏn	ĭndústrĭăl
nònìnfŏrmátiŏnăl	cógnĭtĭve
àrtícŭlàtĕd	cŏmpútĕr

MULTIWORD CONSTRUCTIONS

A: This morning, I've got to chair a *staff meeting.

The term *staff meeting* from our Model Dialog is a type of multiword construction—a compound noun. Multiword constructions are groups of two, or sometimes more, words that have a special meaning together and function like one single word. They also have special stress patterns.

Multiword constructions are common in English. We will be focusing on some of them later on. For now, you need to be familiar with the following types of multiword constructions: compound nouns and multiword verbs.

Compound Nouns

In compound nouns, the first word in the pair ordinarily receives more stress than the second word.

tápe recorder	cópy machine
cóffee house	boók review

Sometimes, compound nouns are hyphenated or written as one word.

light-year	copyright

In *Speechcraft,* we indicate the stress of compound nouns with an asterisk (*). The asterisk directs you to the bottom of the page where you will see a reminder of this special stress pattern so you can begin pronouncing compound nouns properly.

*laser printer	*copyright

---

*compound noun

Phrasal Verbs

A phrasal verb consists of a verb head with one or more particles (e.g., *out, over, at, to, forward*). Sometimes the verb head receives more stress than the particles; sometimes the particle carries the heavier stress.

The position of heavy stress in a phrasal verb depends on many things, including the place of the verb in the text and which particle is involved. For now, you just need to be aware of the different patterns that you may encounter. Here are some examples.

Stress the Particle	Stress the Verb	Stress the First Particle
figure out	look at	run away with
drop off	listen to	look forward to
take over	dispense with	get ahead of

☛ **EXERCISE 4.**   Read the above multiword constructions aloud.

PRACTICE: SYLLABLES, ALTERNATIONS, MAJOR STRESS, MULTIWORD CONSTRUCTIONS

☛ **EXERCISE 1.**   Syllables

1. Listen to your instructor read each word. Write down the number of syllables you hear.

    Example:
       integrate   ___3___

1. leaving	_____	6. fundamental	_____
2. class	_____	7. twenty	_____
3. second	_____	8. professor	_____
4. communicate	_____	9. analysis	_____
5. dialog	_____	10. compel	_____

2. Repeat the words above and tap the syllables as you say them.

☛ **EXERCISE 2.**   Alternations and Major Stress: Definitions

1. At the word level, stressed syllables alternate with unstressed syllables. Alternations are signaled by changes in

    _____   _____   _____

2. There are three possible levels of stress in a word.

Type of Stress	Symbol	Example (listen)
		Mark the stress over the vowel.
_____	_____	superficial
_____	_____	superficial
_____	_____	superficial

☞ **EXERCISE 3.**   Stress and Alternations: Vowel Quality

1. Listen for unstressed syllables. If the syllable is unstressed, write ∪ over it. The first one has been done for you.

      ∪   ∪
   alternations   dissertation   biography

   experimental   connect   symmetrical

   apparent   parallel   nonviolent

2. Listen for stressed syllables. If the syllable is stressed, write S over it. The first one has been done for you.

     S   S
   alternations   magnitude   confrontational

   solution   assignment   confidence

   academic   correlation   parameters

3. Listen to the words in items 1 and 2 above. Put a stress mark (′) over the syllable containing the major stress. The first one has been done for you.

   alternátions

4. Repeat the above words aloud. Remember to use stretched-out, higher pitched, full vowels on the stressed syllables. Use quick, lower pitched, reduced vowels on the unstressed syllables.

☞ **EXERCISE 4.**   Multiword Constructions

1. In a compound noun, which word in the pair usually receives more stress?

   _____

2. Read the following compound nouns aloud.

English department	phone number	disk drive
bookmark	lifestyle	paper clip
area code	study session	Web page

3. Read the following phrasal verbs aloud.

Stress the Particle	**Stress the Verb**	**Stress the First Particle**
find out	learn from	keep up with
come in	think about	stay away from
go over	ask for	brush up on

BEYOND WORDS: OVERVIEW OF THE DISCOURSE LEVEL

PATTERNS

The pronunciation of English occurs at three major levels: sounds, words, and phrases. Phrases, or message units, combine to create discourse. In this lesson, we are going to introduce the pronunciation features of discourse. We will cover each topic in more detail in future chapters.

Why study the pronunciation of English discourse?

In English discourse, a great deal of meaning is signaled through pronunciation. In particular, a listener counts on a speaker to use pronunciation to

- signal where meaningful groups of words begin and end,
- maintain the expected English-style rhythm by carrying the beat on certain words in the message,
- draw attention to important information in the message by putting prominent stress on a particular word or words, and
- convey other kinds of meaning through the use of different vocal melodies.

So we study the sound of English discourse because there are certain agreed-upon pronunciation rules that speakers and listeners must follow if they want to send oral messages back and forth. If you have good control of these rules, listeners will understand what you are trying to say to them, and you will understand what speakers are trying to say to you.

What will be covered in "Beyond Words: Overview of the Discourse Level"?

You will be introduced to the following concepts.

> English discourse is organized into message units.
> Message units are characterized by:
> Rhythm, Primary Stress, and Intonation.

MESSAGE UNITS

Message Units		
Rhythm	Primary Stress	Intonation

What is a message unit?

In spoken English discourse, the message of a speaker is divided into phrases, or groups of words that belong together. We call these phrases **message units,** because they consist of groups of words that belong to one unit in the mind of the speaker. Often a message unit consists of one short sentence, but it can also be just a part of a sentence.

The division between message units is often indicated by a brief pause, as well as by several other features that are presented in more detail later. However, there are some important points to keep in mind.

1. A message unit is the most basic unit of English discourse.
2. The end of a sentence is always the end of a message unit. In *Speechcraft,* we will mark other message units with a bar symbol (|). You can see how the bar is used in this example from the Model Dialog.

    B: This morning, | I'm finishing a review of an article, | and I'm chairing a *staff meeting.

3. A message unit usually consists of a grammatical unit, e.g., prepositional phrases, noun phrases, etc. The groupings, however, do not have to be the same from speaker to speaker. For example, all of the following are acceptable message units.

    Our first step is to isolate the variable | on one side of the equal sign.
    Our first step | is to isolate the variable | on one side of the equal sign.
    Our first step | is to isolate the variable | on one side | of the equal sign.

---

*compound noun

4. Message units may depend on the meaning of the speaker. For example, the following sentence can be divided into message units in more than one way, depending on the speaker's meaning.

    At Cornell, | I studied math and physics for one semester.
    At Cornell, | I studied math | and physics for one semester.

The speaker tells the listener which meaning is intended by signaling through pronunciation where each message unit stops.

How is pronunciation a part of message units?

In English discourse, a typical message unit contains three important features of pronunciation.

- Rhythm (marked ○ • ○ • ○)
- Primary stress (marked ●)
- Intonation (marked with lines).

    Example:

    Maybe you can help me finish these graphs.

☛ **EXERCISE 1.**   Read the examples in points 2, 3, and 4 above. Pause briefly at each bar symbol (|). Do not pause within the message units.

Now we will take a closer look at rhythm, primary stress, and intonation.

PHRASE RHYTHM

Message Units		
Rhythm	Primary Stress	Intonation
Alternations **Linking** **Trimming**		

What are alternations?

English message units have a regular rhythm created by the **alternations of stressed and unstressed words.** The heavier stresses occur at approximately **regular intervals of time.** The weaker stressed syllables are squeezed in between the heavier stressed syllables to facilitate this regular rhythm.

☞ **EXERCISE 2.**   a. Listen to this line from the Model Dialog.
                b. Listen again and tap the rhythm of the heavier stresses
                   (marked with ○ and ●).
                c. Say the line three times, saying the unstressed syllables
                   quickly and the heavier stressed syllables more fully.

     ●   ○   ● ● ● ●
B: I'm r e a l ly in a r u s h.

The alternations of stressed and unstressed words are signaled by changes in vowel length, vowel quality, and voice pitch.

	Stressed Words	**Unstressed Words**
vowel length	stretched out	quick
vowel quality	full	reduced
voice pitch	higher	lower

In unstressed words the vowels are often quick, whereas in stressed words, at least one vowel is stretched out. The vowels in unstressed words are reduced vowels; in stressed words at least one syllable is full. And unstressed words are often lower in voice pitch than stressed words.

☞ **EXERCISE 3.**   Say this part of the Model Dialog with an evenly timed, regular rhythm. Stretch out the vowel of the words marked with ○ and ●. Squeeze the words marked • in between the heavy stresses.

         •   •   ○ • •   ●

A: Do you need any help?

        ○ • •   •   ○   • ○•   •   ●

B: Maybe you could help me finish these graphs.

Which words are usually stressed and which words are usually unstressed?

In general, stressed words are either **content words** or **loud function words.** Unstressed words are **soft function words.** So content words and loud function words alternate with soft function words, and their differences in stress create a regular rhythm.

Stressed (stretched out, full vowel, higher pitch)		Unstressed (quick, reduced vowel, lower pitch)
Content Words	**Loud Function Words**	**Soft Function Words**
Nouns Verbs Adjectives Adverbs	question words demonstrative pronouns negatives	to be pronouns and other proforms articles auxiliaries prepositions conjunctions, etc.

☞ **EXERCISE 4.**   a. Which words are stressed and which words are unstressed in this part of the Model Dialog? Mark the content words and loud function words with ○. Mark the soft function words with •.
           b. Read the line aloud using regular rhythm.

B: You'll never believe it. It's "How to manage your time."

How else are alternations created?

In addition to reduced vowels in unstressed words, English has other ways to help create the characteristic rhythmic timing of spoken English.

Linking is one way to squeeze the sounds between heavier stresses. So that no time is lost between the words in a message unit, native speakers link the final sound of each word with the beginning sound of the next word.

In this part of the Model Dialog, linking (marked ‿) within the message units produces a smooth connection between words.

> *A:* No‿problem. Are‿you‿always‿so‿busy?
> *B:* Well,‿today‿I'm‿especially‿busy. This‿morning, | I'm‿finishing‿ a‿review‿of‿an‿article, | and‿I'm‿chairing‿a‿*staff‿meeting. Then‿I‿need‿to‿get‿ready‿to‿present‿a‿seminar.

Trimming is another way to keep the timing of spoken English. That is, in certain environments, vowel and consonant sounds are eliminated from the flow of speech in order to allow the speaker to pronounce the next stressed syllable on the next beat.

There are many types of trimming that we will explore later. For now, take a look at one common type of trimming—contractions.

I would	→	I'd
are not	→	aren't
I am	→	I'm
where is	→	where's
it is	→	it's
we will	→	we'll

In contractions, sounds and/or syllables are eliminated. This helps native speakers to produce regular alternations between stressed and unstressed words more easily.

☛ **EXERCISE 5.**   a. Circle the contractions in the part of the Model Dialog just above.
  b. Practice reading the dialog aloud, focusing on linking (smooth connections within message units) and trimming (using contractions, not full forms).

---

*compound noun

PRIMARY STRESS

Message Units		
Rhythm	**Primary Stress**	Intonation
	One word: lengthening and pitch move	

What is primary stress?

In addition to rhythm, every English message unit typically has one most promi-nent stressed word. We call the most prominent stress **primary stress.** In *Speechcraft,* primary stress is marked with a solid circle (●). Primary stress is signaled by the following.

- Vowel length. The vowel in this word is more stretched out than the other vowels in the message unit. If there is more than one syllable in this word, the syllable containing the major stress receives the primary stress.
- Pitch move. The syllable that has primary stress will suddenly change pitch—sometimes higher, sometimes lower—in comparison with the previ-ous syllables. When it moves higher, it is called a *pitch jump.* When it moves lower, it is called a *pitch drop.* The pitch move is indicated by the solid line.

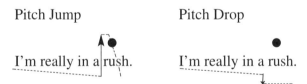

Pitch Jump　　　　　　Pitch Drop

I'm really in a rush.　　　I'm really in a rush.

Where does the primary stress go?

Notice the location of the primary stress in this portion of the Model Dialog.

                         ●

B:　I need to get ready to present a seminar.

              ●

A:　What's the topic of the seminar?

                 ●   ●

B:　You'll never believe it. It's "How to manage your time."

Primary stress is often placed

- on a content word (the words *seminar, topic, believe,* and *time* are all content words);
- at or near the end of a message unit;
- on the new information in a message unit.

To see the third point most clearly, look at A's turn. Here, *seminar* is old information because it has already been mentioned by B. Therefore, *topic,* which is new information in the conversation, receives primary stress.

●

B: I <u>need to get ready to present a seminar</u>.

●

A: <u>What's the topic of</u> the seminar?

In *Speechcraft,* we often underline new information and parenthesize old information to help us identify it. In the message units below, the new information is underlined and old information is parenthesized.

●

B: (I)'<u>m really in a rush</u>.

●

A: <u>Do</u> (you) <u>need any help</u>?

Notice that nearly every word carries new information. When more than one word in a message unit carries new information, we put the primary stress on **the last content word in the new information,** in this case, *rush* and *help*. Later you will see why pronouns are usually old information.

We will discuss, practice, and refine these generalizations for primary stress later.

☞ **EXERCISE 6.**   Practice reading this portion of the Model Dialog aloud, focusing on using a more stretched-out vowel sound and a pitch jump or pitch drop at the primary stress.

●

A: Are you always so busy?

●   ●

B: Well, today I'm especially busy. This morning, | I'm finishing a review of

●   ●

an article, | and I'm chairing a *staff meeting. Then I need to get ready to

●

present a seminar.

●

A: What's the topic of the seminar?

●   ●

B: You'll never believe it. It's "How to manage your time."

―――――――――

*compound noun

INTONATION

Message Units		
Rhythm	Primary Stress	**Intonation**
		Pitch move after Primary Stress

Voice pitch is present in every syllable we say. It varies with our rhythm across a message unit (pitch alternation). It moves abruptly with our primary stress (pitch move). It rises or falls after our pitch move (intonation). Together, all of these pitch changes are called **melody.**

What is intonation?

The **intonation** part of a melody refers to the direction of the pitch *after* the pitch move. Intonation can fall, rise, or combine a fall and a rise (fall-rise), as shown in these examples with a pitch move up (pitch jump).

Falling intonation (↓)

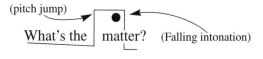

Rising intonation (↑)

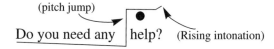

Fall-rise intonation (↘)

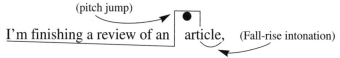

In general, intonation helps signal the boundary of a message unit, lets listeners know when they can take a turn at talking, and can also carry certain kinds of meaning, like "This sentence is incomplete," or "I have more to say," or "This is a special question."

The following exercises illustrate the three different intonations that follow a pitch jump. Later, we will look at intonation following a pitch drop as well.

☛ **EXERCISE 7.**
a. Listen to the intonation patterns of the Model Dialog. Notice how the intonation lines match the pitch of the voice.
b. Listen to the dialog again, moving your hand to reflect the contours of the voice. (Pretend you are a musical conductor.)
c. Repeat the Model Dialog aloud, focusing on the intonation.

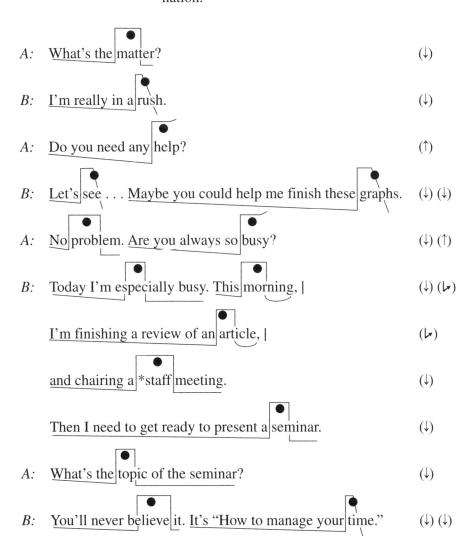

A: What's the matter? (↓)

B: I'm really in a rush. (↓)

A: Do you need any help? (↑)

B: Let's see . . . Maybe you could help me finish these graphs. (↓) (↓)

A: No problem. Are you always so busy? (↓) (↑)

B: Today I'm especially busy. This morning, | (↓) (↳)

I'm finishing a review of an article, | (↳)

and chairing a *staff meeting. (↓)

Then I need to get ready to present a seminar. (↓)

A: What's the topic of the seminar? (↓)

B: You'll never believe it. It's "How to manage your time." (↓) (↓)

*compound noun

☞ **EXERCISE 8.**   a. Listen to the intonation patterns of the following dialog.
b. Circle ↓ for falling, ↑ for rising, and ↳ for a fall-rise intonation.

Situation. Two colleagues talking

	Falling	**Rising**	**Fall-Rise**
● *A:* Working on your paper?	↓	↑	↳
● *B:* I'm trying, |	↓	↑	↳
● but it's taking forever.	↓	↑	↳
● *A:* What do you have left?	↓	↑	↳
● *B:* The results,	↓	↑	↳
● the conclusions,	↓	↑	↳
● and the references.	↓	↑	↳
● *A:* You finished analyzing the data?	↓	↑	↳
● *B:* Yes, and it's fascinating.	↓	↑	↳
● Take a look.	↓	↑	↳

PRACTICE

☞ **EXERCISE**   Interview
                      a. Mark the content words and loud function words with ○.
                      b. Mark the function words with •.
                      c. Mark the primary stress with ●.
                      d. Interview your partner.
                      e. Write down and mark the stress on the answers.

         ○   •   ●

A: What's your name?   *B:* My name's _____.

A: What do you like to be called? *B:* I like to be called _____.

A: What profession (or area of

     specialization) are you in?   *B:* I'm in _____.

A: Why are you taking this class? *B:* _____

                              _____ .

A: What do you like to do for fun? *B:* I like to _____.

DISCOURSE LEVEL TOPICS

In Discourse Level Topics, students focus on the features that give English discourse its unique rhythm. Because almost all oral communication occurs at the discourse level, all of these topics are crucial for intelligibility.

DISCOURSE FOUNDATIONS

Lessons in Discourse Foundations expand on and provide more practice with the discourse topics introduced in Groundwork. They are "foundations" to the special contexts that are found in Discourse Domains in the workbooks. The following topics are covered in Discourse Foundations.

D-1

MESSAGE UNITS

Speakers help listeners process their message by breaking their utterances into message units. A message unit is a string of words that belong together as one unit in the mind of the speaker. Message units are often separated from each other by a brief pause (|). Each message unit has its own intonation, and most message units have one primary stress.

Example: In today's lesson, | we will look at *message units | and have some practice | marking them in sentences | and using them in speech.

The Composition of Message Units

There is no formula to determine the size or content of a message unit, but the following guidelines are helpful.

1. Message units consist of meaningful grammatical units.

    Example: The first colloquium | will be next Friday.
    NOT: The | first colloquium will be next | Friday.

2. If you want to bring attention to a term, pause briefly just before or just after it.

    Example: Today, I want to discuss an important topic: | *professionalism.*
    A verb that is *transitive* | is a verb that takes an object.

3. The more message units you use, the more emphatic your message sounds. This is because you are highlighting more information that you want to emphasize as important.

---

*compound noun

Compare

> A pause has some power to draw your attention to what the speaker is trying to say.

> A pause has some power | to draw your attention | to what the speaker is trying to say.

Sound Features of Message Units

1. There is often a brief pause at the boundary of a message unit.

   ☞ Listen to this example for the pauses.

   > A pause has some power | to draw your attention | to what the speaker is trying to say.

2. Each message unit usually contains one primary stress.

   ☞ Listen to this example for the primary stresses.

   > ●   ●
   > A pause has some power | to draw your attention | to what the speaker is
   >
   > ●
   > trying to say.

3. Each message unit also has its own intonation pattern. If you have more than one message unit in a statement, the last message unit will usually have falling intonation. In order to indicate that your sentence is not complete, the nonfinal message units should use rising or a fall-rise intonation, which can signal incompleteness.

   ☞ Listen to the intonation in this example.

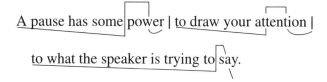

The Sounds within Message Units

1. Within the message units, words are linked smoothly.

    ☞ Listen to this example for linking.

    A_pause_has_some_power | to_draw_your_attention | to_what_the_
    speaker_is_trying_to_say.

2. Within the message units, remember to use rhythmic alternations.

    ☞ Listen to this example for rhythmic alternations.

    • ○   ○ •   ● • • ○   • • ● •   •   ○ • ○ • •
    A pause has some power | to draw your attention | to what the speaker is
    ○•   • ●
    trying to say.

☞ **EXERCISE 1.**   Read the following sentences aloud, focusing on the mes-
                        sage units.

1. A gene | is an element of the *germ plasm | that controls transmission of a
   hereditary characteristic.
2. The gross national product | is the total value | of all the goods and services |
   that are produced by a nation | during a specified period of time.
3. The term geostrophic | refers to a deflective force | caused by the rotation of
   the earth.
4. A phoneme | is the smallest unit of speech | that distinguishes one meaning
   from another | in a given language or dialect.
5. In a meritocracy, | you are chosen or moved ahead | based on your talents or
   personal achievements.
6. A syllogism | is a kind of deductive reasoning | in formal argumentation |
   that consists of a major and minor premise | and a conclusion.
7. *A:*   Is there anyone here who can tell us | how to calculate the mean?
   B: You add up all the scores, | then divide by the total number of scores.

Definitions in items 1–6 adapted by permission. From *Merriam-Webster's Collegiate® Dictionary,*
Tenth Edition © 1979 by Merriam-Webster, Incorporated.

---

*compound noun

☞ **EXERCISE 2.**   In the following passage,
a. Mark the message units with a bar symbol (|).
b. Compare your marks with a partner's. Are they the same? Do they all contain grammatical phrases?
c. Read the passage aloud, following the message units. Try using the "read and look up" technique: Read a message unit silently to yourself, then look up and say it smoothly without looking at the page.

The term *rapport* refers to the relationship that you establish and maintain with your audience. In order to develop rapport during a lecture, you can use a number of strategies. Whenever possible, it's a good idea to learn something about your audience before you begin. That way, your lecture can become more personalized. For instance, the explanations and examples you use could be directly related to the participants' backgrounds. Another way to build rapport is through personal interaction with your audience. If you know their names, you can use them as frequently as possible. Before and after your lecture, casual conversation will make everyone more relaxed and help you and your audience get to know each other. During your lecture, good *eye contact, a sense of humor, and a genuine openness to your audience's questions and ideas will also help you develop a good relationship with them. In general, an enthusiastic and personal approach to both your audience and your *subject matter is the key to establishing and maintaining good rapport.

Three Important Points to Bear in Mind

1. Too many pauses in ungrammatical, unmeaningful places or pauses that are too long can result in serious comprehension problems for listeners.
2. Each message unit usually contains one primary stress. Since listeners use message units as a frame to evaluate new and old information, too many message units (and primary stresses) can result in listeners' being unable to evaluate old and new information adequately.
3. It is not normally best to use long sentences in spoken English, even if you divide them into shorter message units. If you use long sentences, you will sound more like a textbook than a human being, and your listeners will have difficulty processing what you say. When giving a lecture or presentation, it is best to speak spontaneously, with shorter message units, rather than to

*compound noun

read. If you do read, your text should reflect natural spoken English—including message unit divisions.

Too much: A university is an institution of higher learning with facilities for teaching and research and includes resources for graduate, professional, and undergraduate study, all of which grant postsecondary degrees.

Better: A university is an institution of higher learning | with facilities for teaching and research | and includes resources for graduate, | professional, | and undergraduate study, | all of which grant postsecondary degrees.

Best: A university is an institution of higher learning. | At a university, | you can teach and do research. You can also get a postsecondary degree | at the graduate, | professional, | or undergraduate level.

☛ **EXERCISE 3.**   Choose a topic below and prepare to speak about it for two minutes.
   a. Write out the key sentences of your talk, marking shorter, spoken message units as demonstrated above.
   b. Practice your talk, focusing on the rhythm and melody in the message units.
   c. Tape-record your talk.

Topic 1. Describe the role that computers play in your life.
Topic 2. Does watching television help you learn English? Why or why not?
Topic 3. Describe your favorite book.
Topic 4. Discuss why you chose your profession.
Topic 5. Describe your favorite teacher.
Topic 6. Discuss what you expect to be doing fifteen years from now.

D-2

RHYTHM—ALTERNATIONS

☞ **EXERCISE 1.** Listening to Alternations

  a. Listen to the rhythmic alternations in the following
     maxim.
  b. Mark the heavier stressed words with ○.
  c. Listen again and mark the lesser stressed words with •.

In prosperous fortunes be modest and wise,

The greatest may fall and the lowest may rise.
                            —Benjamin Franklin, *Poor Richard's Almanac*

Alternations

The rhythm of English is characterized by the fairly regular alternations of
stressed and unstressed words and syllables.

1. The heavier stresses occur at approximately regular intervals of time. The
   weaker unstressed syllables are squeezed in between the heavier,
   stretched-out, stressed syllables.
2. This characteristic rhythm is signaled by alternations in

     a. length (stretched out or quick),
     b. vowel quality (full or reduced), and
     c. intensity (louder or quieter).

3. In general, heavier stressed syllables are in content words or loud function words; unstressed and weaker stressed syllables are in soft function
   words and in other parts of content words (see the Phrase Rhythm section
   in Groundwork G-4).

☛ **EXERCISE 2.**   Practicing Alternations
a. Listen to the rhythmic alternations in the following maxims.
b. Repeat the rhymes and tap a hand or foot with the heavy stresses.

◯ • • ◯ • ◯ • • ◯
Early to bed and early to rise

◯ • ◯ • ◯ • • ◯
makes us healthy, wealthy, and wise.

◯ • • ◯ •
Nothing but Money

• ◯ • • ◯ •
is sweeter than Honey.

—Benjamin Franklin, *Poor Richard's Almanac*

1. In the maxims in Exercise 2, the content words and loud function words are marked with ◯, and the soft function words are marked with •.
2. To make the heavy stresses stand out prominently, vowels in the other syllables will typically be quick, quiet, and reduced to /ə/, /ər/, /i/, /u/, /o/.

Sometimes, however, these other syllables have quick and quiet vowels that are **not** reduced to /ə/, /ər/, /i/, /u/, /o/. Nevertheless, it is still important to squeeze these syllables so they contrast with the stressed syllables to create the rhythm. Watch for these additional categories.

- The following single-syllable soft function words do not have reduced vowels.

be	she	my	by	while	should	on
he	we	I	down	so	could	off
me	they	may	out	do	would	

- Two-syllable soft function words have one full-vowel syllable and one reduced-vowel syllable, e.g., *about, beneath, because, either, around, whether, over, under, below*. Both syllables are spoken quickly and quietly.
- Even the minor-stressed vowels in content words are squeezed by being spoken quickly and quietly, even though they have full vowels, e.g., *stóplìght, nótepàd.*

☞ **EXERCISE 3.**   Regular Alternations
a. Mark the content words and loud function words with
○ in the following maxims.
b. Say the rhymes aloud, tapping your hand or foot to feel
the regular beat.

Hope of gain

lessens pain.

A quiet Conscience sleeps in Thunder,

but Rest and Guilt live far asunder.

("Asunder" means "apart.")

A slip of the foot you may soon recover,

But a slip of the Tongue you may never get over.

("Get over" is a phrasal verb, so "over" is stressed.)
Benjamin Franklin, *Poor Richard's Almanac*

☞ **EXERCISE 4.**   Alternations in Sentences
a. Say the following sentences aloud.
b. Keep the heavy beats regular as you add unstressed syllables.

Friends   need   help.
My friends have   needed   help.
My friends have been needing some help.
All of my friends have been needing some help.
All of my friends have been needing some help with their work.

Proposal's   due   Friday.
Our proposal's   due   Friday.
Our proposal's   due on Friday.
Our proposal should have been due on Friday.
Our proposal should have been due on Friday at the latest.

NOTE: Word stress contributes directly to phrase stress. If you say "pró-
posals" instead of "propósals," or "Fridaý" instead of "Fríday," the
rhythm of the entire phrase is disturbed. So using correct word stress is
essential for good overall rhythm.

☛ **EXERCISE 5.**   Alternations in Signposts
           a. Mark the content words and loud function words with ○.
           b. Say the phrases and sentences aloud, tapping your hand
             or foot to feel the regular beat.

These phrases and sentences are structuring devices or "signposts" commonly used in lectures to let your audience know how what you are about to say fits into the overall structure of your lecture or presentation.

Introducing a Topic

The topic for today is (enzymes).

What we need to cover next is
     (enzymes).

Today we're going to talk about
     (enzymes).

Giving Examples

For example, . . .

Let me give you an example (of an
     enzyme).

For instance, . . .

Restating, Paraphrasing

Let me repeat that.

I'll say it again so you're sure to
     remember it.

Let me say that in another way.

In other words, . . .

To put it another way, . . .

Getting off and Back onto the Topic

By the way, . . .

It's a little off the topic, but . . .

Anyway, as I was saying, . . .

Now back to what we were talking
     about.

Emphasizing Points

I want to make this clear.

This is an important point.

Be sure you get this point.
     It's important.

Concluding

In conclusion, . . .

So let's see if we can summarize.

What can we conclude for today?

☛ **EXERCISE 6.**   Alternations in Your Own Speech
  a. Choose two of the phrases in the signpost categories.
  b. For each phrase, create a short passage using a topic from your own field of study.
  c. Say the passage aloud three times, using rhythmic alternations.

Example: A lecture on physiology

> So let's see if we can summarize. Today we started talking about motor control. And we saw how some movements are probably genetically defined and others are learned through practice.

Example: A lecture on Spanish literature

> . . . So if you are interested in romantic poets, Gustavo Adolfo Bécquer would be a good place to start. Now, back to what we were talking about: realism in nineteenth-century literature.

RHYTHM—LINKING

> Linking refers to the smooth connection between words in English. Within a message unit, there are no breaks between words. That is, adjacent words are spoken as if they were one long word. Linking also occurs within words, to connect separate syllables smoothly.

You learned in Groundwork that one characteristic of English rhythm is its regular timing. Native speakers use linking to help maintain the even timing of their rhythm by eliminating breaks between words. Remember that breaks can occur between message units—these are natural pauses in extended speech. But within message units, smooth linking occurs everywhere, between all words. Here are some of the most important types of linking.

Consonant-to-Vowel Linking. C‿V

Link the last consonant sound of the first word to the first vowel sound of the next word.

☛ Listen to the linking.

an easy test	(you will hear "knees")
figure out	(you will hear "rout")
It's like ashes.	(you will hear "cash")
some iodine	(you will hear "my")

☞ Read the following words and phrases aloud. Concentrate on smooth linking.

1. the speaker's attitude
2. to check in
3. some other ones
4. *homework assignment
5. writing essays
6. horizontal axis
7. one example
8. in October
9. *lab experiment
10. University of Illinois
11. an assumption
12. of lesser importance
13. *time interval
14. with minor implications
15. going over
16. an algorithm

Vowel-to-Vowel Linking. V‿V

Vowel-to-vowel linking occurs not only across words but also within words, to join separate syllables smoothly. Certain vowels are linked by inserting a brief /w/ or /y/ sound between them.

☞ Listen to the linking.

Across Words	Within Words
go on	coauthored
thorough analysis	altruistic
the day afterward	remediation
carry out	triangular

1. /w/-glided vowels at the end of a word have a prominent /w/ to link them to another upcoming vowel (V). The following vowel sounds work this way.

	Across Words	Within Words
/uw/ + /w/ + V	do algebra	intuition
/ow/ + /w/ + V	go into	coincidence
/aw/ + /w/ + V	how interesting	allowing

---

*compound noun

2. /y/-glided vowels at the end of a word have a prominent /y/ to link them to another upcoming vowel (V). The following vowel sounds work this way.

	Across Words	Within Words
/iy/ + /y/ + V	see Oliver	variation
/ey/ + /y/ + V	say anything	laity
/ay/ + /y/ + V	I asked	diagonal
/ɔy/ + /y/ + V	enjoy arguing	annoying

☞ Read the following words and phrases aloud. Concentrate on smooth linking.

Across Words		Within Words	
1. two algorithms	knew about it	situation	renewable
2. so interesting	show up	coagulate	flowing
3. Now it's over.	allow individuals	endowing	plowing
4. three offices	be available	geography	creative
5. today after class	stay awake	chaotic	payable
6. my efforts	try other ones	biology	triangulate
7. a Troy ounce	annoy everyone	enjoyable	destroyer

Consonant-to-Same-Consonant Linking. C‿C$_{same}$

When two identical consonant sounds come together, they are pronounced as one somewhat stretched-out sound.

☞ Listen to the linking.

lead discussions   some money   *business strategy

☞ Read the following words and phrases aloud. Concentrate on smooth linking.

1. It's about time.
2. a full liter
3. a good design
4. It looks strange.
5. a tough four hours
6. some music
7. Mike's scholarship
8. You look confused.
9. evaluate two articles
10. a nice synthesis
11. the square root
12. It's smaller.

A pair of identical consonant spellings within words are also usually pronounced as one sound but are *not* stretched out, e.g., *caller, missing, effort.*

*compound noun

Consonant-Stop-to-Different-Consonant-Stop Linking. $C_{stop}\smile C_{stop}$

When two different consonant stops come together, we change the point of articulation without releasing air between the two. This includes cases where the second consonant is a nasal, which stops the air in the mouth.

☞ Listen to the linking.

Across Words	**Within Words**
like music	ca**pt**ivity
a hard night	ca**tn**ap
a good memory	a**dm**it
look polished	a**ct**ivate
keep testing	dece**pt**ive
enthusiastic teams	defe**ct**or
absorb chemicals	o**bt**use

☞ Read the following words and phrases aloud. Concentrate on smooth linking.

1. the right moment
2. stick together
3. directive
4. keep notes
5. subcategories
6. top-down processing
7. stop trying
8. joint probability
9. abdicated
10. apartment
11. pop quiz
12. specific times

Consonant-to-Similar-Consonant Linking. $C\smile C_{similar}$

When two different adjacent consonants are made in the same, or nearly the same, place in the mouth, there is a change of articulation or voicing, but there is no break.

☞ Listen to the linking.

come back   one difference   the third line

☛ Read the following words and phrases aloud. Concentrate on smooth linking.

1. I'll decide.	7. a strong conclusion
2. has suggested	8. improve further
3. It stopped.	9. has time
4. full responsibility	10. read several novels
5. the same word	11. a wrong guess
6. a *turn signal	12. a wool suit

This type of linking within words can usually be done easily, e.g., *embassy, undeniable, needless.*

☛ **EXERCISE 1.** Idioms
a. Read the following idioms aloud. Concentrate on smooth linking.
b. Explain to a partner what you think the idiom means.

a *couch potato	pie in the sky	to let sleeping dogs lie
a wet blanket	the concrete jungle	to go out on a limb
a *stick-in-the-mud	a heart to heart talk	to sleep on it

☛ **EXERCISE 2.** Famous Quotations
a. Read the following famous quotes aloud. Concentrate on smooth linking.
b. Explain to a partner what you think the quote means.

A teacher affects eternity; he can never tell where his influence stops.

—Henry Adams

I never did anything worth doing by accident, nor did any of my inventions come by accident; they came by work.

—Attributed to Thomas A. Edison

Every language is a temple, in which the soul of those who speak it is enshrined.

—Oliver Wendell Holmes, Sr.

---

*compound noun

☞ **EXERCISE 3.** Giving Directions
a. Read the following street and building names aloud. Concentrate on smooth linking.
b. Choose two places on the map and explain to a partner how to get from one place to the other.

	Cutlass Street	Branch Street	Three Oaks Road	Clark Boulevard	Illinois Avenue
4th Avenue	Cameo Insurance		Environmental Lab		
5th Avenue					ATM Machine
6th Avenue		State Bank		Skylark Café	
7th Avenue	May's Store				

☞ **EXERCISE 4.** In your academic or professional setting, listen for the special types of linking.

$$C\smile V \quad V\smile V \quad C\smile C_{same} \quad C_{stop}\smile C_{stop} \quad C\smile C_{similar}$$

a. Write down three or four phrases you hear.
b. Identify the type(s) of linking that occur in those phrases.
c. Read each phrase aloud, concentrating on smooth linking.

☛ **EXERCISE 5.**   Write five sentences you would use in your academic or professional setting.

a. Identify the type(s) of linking that occur in those phrases.

$$C\smile V \qquad V\smile V \qquad C\smile C_{same} \qquad C_{stop}\smile C_{stop} \qquad C\smile C_{similar}$$

b. Read each sentence aloud, concentrating on smooth linking.

1. _____

2. _____

3. _____

4. _____

5. _____

D-4

RHYTHM—TRIMMING

Trimming refers to the elimination of certain vowel and consonant sounds in natural English discourse. Native speakers regularly "trim" certain vowel and consonant sounds in order to help maintain the even timing of their rhythm.

- Trimming makes a direct contribution to nativelike rhythm. Therefore, trimming in the right places does not make a speaker sound sloppy or uneducated but rather natural and fluent.
- Trimming can only occur in certain word patterns. It is inappropriate to omit any other vowels and consonants.
- Most (not all) trimming is optional in speech, but you must learn to understand spoken English that has it.

Contractions

Contractions consist of words joined to make one word by trimming consonants and/or vowels. The missing sounds are marked in spelling with an apostrophe. Usually contractions are made up of two function words.

In spoken English, contractions are much more common than their full forms.

's Contractions (with *is, us, has*)	
How's it going? (How is)	She's been waiting for it. (She has)
There's a package for Maria. (There is)	Let's give it to her. (Let us)

A: When's the conference?
B: Let's see . . . It's been postponed. It's May 9.

'd Contractions (with *had, would, did*)

I'd give it a try. (I would)   We'd seen it before. (We had)
How'd you do that? (How did)   That'd be great. (That would)

A: Where'd you get that book?
B: At Follett's. I'd been on the *waiting list for ages.
A: Do you think it'd be OK if I borrowed it?

've Contractions (with *have*)

How've you been? (How have)   It could've been better. (could have)
We've tried everything. (We have)   They've been waiting for it. (They have)

A: Where've you been?
B: I've been at the library.
A: You should've called.

---

n't Contractions (with *not*)

You didn't get my message. (did not)   I can't find my files. (can not)
I haven't checked my *e-mail. (have not)   It wouldn't take long. (would not)

A: Didn't you hear about Ted?
B: I haven't heard anything. What's the scoop?
A: He said he wouldn't work overtime any more, so he was fired.
B: I don't believe it!

---

*compound noun

'll Contractions (with *will*)	
It'll be fantastic. (It will)	She'll really be pleased. (She will)
I'll tell her. (I will)	You'll have to rewrite it. (You will)

A: Who'll volunteer to go first?
B: We'll go—ready or not.
A: That'll be fine.

're Contractions (with *are*)	
You're improving. (You are)	We're making progress. (We are)

A: We're going to have to recalculate those figures.
B: I think you're right. They don't make any sense.
A: They're just too low to be reasonable.

☞ **EXERCISE 1.**   Read the above phrases and dialogs aloud.

Vowel Trimming

Some words lose a vowel sound and therefore lose a syllable. This trimming of a syllable occurs in words that have the following pattern.

		Stressed Syllable		Unstressed Syllable		l/n/r Unstressed Syllable
privilege	→	prív	-	ĭ	-	lĕge
business	→	bús	-	ĭ	-	nĕss
interest	→	ínt	-	ĕ	-	rĕst

Some other words that follow this pattern are the following.

l	*n*	*r*
accidéntally	awákening	ádmirable
anómalous	cábinet	áverage
báchelor	cárdinal	brávery
cháncellor	críminal	cámera
coúnselor	deáfening	consíderable
customárily	définite	córporal
désolate	évening	compúlsory
espécially	excéptional	cúltural
éxcellent	fórtunately	discóvery
fámily	góvernor	dóctoral
fínally	inténtional	eláborate
léveling	lístening	évery
líbelous	loósening	fáctory
márvelous	órdinal	gállery
momentárily	nátional	géneral
necessárily	ópening	hístory
ordinárily	oríginal	mémory
páneling	pérsonal	númerous
primárily	prísoners	óperative
quárreler	rátional	recóvery
símilar	stráightening	sálary
tráveler	tradítional	séparate

☛ **EXERCISE 2.**
    a. Mark out the trimmed vowel in each word above.
       Example: accidéntally awákening ádmirable
    b. Then read each word aloud.

☛ **EXERCISE 3.**
    a. Choose three words from the list of general academic terms below that follow this trimming pattern.
    b. Construct five or more sentences containing your chosen words.
    c. Mark out the trimmed vowel in each word. Example: counsélor.
    d. Then read each sentence aloud.

anómaly	consíderable	dífference	dífferent
dóminant	líberal	líteral	márginal
réference	súmmary	tradítional	

Consonant Trimming

1. *h-* pronouns and *h-* auxiliary verbs. When they are in unstressed, noninitial position in a message unit, these words may lose /h/. When this happens, the preceding vowel or consonant links to the vowel after the trimmed /h/.

> *h-* pronouns: *he, his, him, her*
> *h-* auxiliary verbs: *have, has, had*

> Examples: Is he going? (Is **h**e going?) vs. He's going.
> We showed him around. (We showed **h**im around.)
> We'll see her later. (We'll see **h**er later.)
> The students had gone. (The students **h**ad gone.)
> We know his address. (We know **h**is address.)
> Where is he? (Where is **h**e?)
> I enjoy her lectures. (I enjoy **h**er lectures.)
> The play had been canceled. (The play **h**ad been canceled.)

2. Final consonant clusters that include /t/ or /d/. Consonant clusters consisting of any consonant plus /t/ or /d/ may lose the /t/ or /d/ sound before another consonant. Special cases are noted below. When the /t/ or /d/ is lost, the remaining consonant must be linked to the next sound.

C + / t / + C	C + / d / + C
the first sign	He used several stamps.
the last page	send the letter
She kept staring.	saved stamps
She looked confused.	found someone

Within Words

mostly	profoundly
correctness	friendship
Christmas	boldface (a typeface)

However, /t/ and /d/ are *not* trimmed in the following environments.

- Before vowels (V) or *w, h, y,* or *r*

C + /t/ + V, *w, h, y, r*	**C + /d/ + V, *w, h, y, r***
the firs**t** round	He use**d** way too much.
the las**t** year	sen**d** out for pizza
She kep**t** out of it.	save**d** envelopes
She looke**d** around.	foun**d** Heather

- In clusters *lt, nt, rt,* and *rd* (or *red*)

***l, n, r* + /t/ + C**	***r(e)* + /d/ + C**
guil**t** by association	hear**d** several stories
ben**t** the rules	barre**d** from practice
hur**t** my hand	

Within Words

faul**t**less	aler**t**ness
recen**t**ly	har**d**ship
shor**t**-listed	good-nature**dl**y

NOTE: The /d/ in the word *and* is almost always trimmed, even before vowels. Often the vowel of *and* is also trimmed, and only the /n/ is pronounced.

rises and falls	→	rises 'n' falls
paper and pens	→	paper 'n' pens
bits and bytes	→	bits 'n' bytes
memorize and repeat	→	memorize 'n' repeat
black and white	→	black 'n' white

☞ **EXERCISE 4.**   Read aloud the words and phrases in consonant trimming.

☞ **EXERCISE 5.**   Questions and Answers
      a. In the following sentences, identify words that have trimmed vowels and/or consonants.
      b. With a partner, ask and answer the questions.

1. What are some topics for *small talk that interest you?
2. Is higher education a right or a privilege? Why?
3. What are some ways you can improve your listening skills?
4. What are you going to do this evening?
5. What's the average salary for graduates in your field?
6. What's one cultural difference between your country and the United States?
7. What's your idea of the perfect job?
8. What are the characteristics of an excellent friendship?
9. Who's a prominent figure in the history of your country? Describe him/her.
10. What's your first childhood memory?

☞ **EXERCISE 6.**   Explaining a Graph
   a. In the following graph, identify words and phrases that have trimmed vowels and/or consonants.
   b. Read the words and phrases aloud.
   c. Explain the graph to a partner. Be sure to use the full names of the airlines, not the initials.

Total Number of Customers per Quarter for Airline Companies

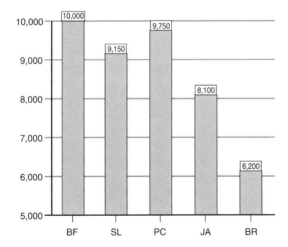

BF = Best Flight
SL = The Sky's the Limit
PC = Privileged Class
JA = Just Average Airlines
BR = Bob's and Rob's

---

*compound noun

D-5

PRIMARY STRESS—NEW INFORMATION IN CONTENT WORDS

☛ **EXERCISE 1.** There is usually one primary stress in each message unit.
a. Listen to your instructor read the following passage.
b. Mark the primary stresses with ●.
c. Try to figure out for yourself what factors influence the placement of primary stress.

We use the *pH meter | to measure the acidity or alkalinity of compounds. If the pH value is lower than seven, | then it's an acid. If the value is larger than seven, | then it's a base. If the value is exactly seven, | we call this a neutral compound. For example, | water is a neutral compound. (Adapted with permission from Yang Zhang, oral presentation, ESL 404, UIUC, 1992.)

In Groundwork, you learned that primary stress consists of vowel lengthening and a pitch move. Recall that you can have a pitch jump or a pitch drop.

Pitch Jump   Pitch Drop

then it's a base.   then it's a base.

Where does primary stress go?

In order to determine which word in a message unit receives primary stress, it is important to understand the concepts of **new and old information.**

---

*compound noun

New Information

- New information refers to words or ideas in a message unit that are new to the conversation. They are words not used before or ideas not already obvious to the speakers.
- New information is often found at the end of a message unit.
- New information can be in one word or in a string of words.
- The primary stress will fall on one word in the new information, often on a content word.

Content Words

nouns
verbs
adjectives
adverbs

- In this example from above, all of the words in this message unit carry new information.

●

If the pH value is lower than seven, |

Old Information

- Old information refers to words in a message unit that have already been a part of the conversation or to what is shared in the speaking situation.
- Old information is often found in pronouns. Pronouns refer to something or someone mentioned before or known from the context.
- Old information does not attract primary stress because it is not part of the message emphasized by the speaker.
- In this example from above, old information is in parentheses.

●

(If the value is) exactly (seven), |

In new information, primary stress goes on the last content word.

☛ **EXERCISE 2.**   Read the passage on the pH meter aloud.

☞ EXERCISE 3.   In B's turn in the following dialogs,
a. Underline the new information.
b. Put parentheses around old information.
c. In the answer to the question, mark the primary stress on the new information.
d. Read each dialog aloud.

Example:

                                  ●

A: Who's the head of your department?

              ●

B: <u>Dr. Taylor</u>('s the head.)
(<u>Taylor</u> is the last content word in the new information.)

Situation 1. Class discussion

                         ●

A: What kind of triangle is this?

B: It's a right triangle.

Situation 2. At an interview

                                           ●

A: What was your major when you were in college?

B: Physics was my major.

                        ●

A: What was your area of specialty?

B: Nuclear physics.

Situation 3. Two colleagues talking about their work

                                 ●

A: Do you have any ideas for your next project?

B: I have a few ideas. But nothing very interesting.

☛ **EXERCISE 4.**   In the following dialogs and passages,
a. Underline the new information.
b. Put parentheses around old information.
c. Mark the primary stress on the new information.
d. Read each passage aloud.

Example 1:

A: How would you compare a lecture and a discussion?
B: I think a lecture's more formal than a discussion.

                                                  ●

A: How would (you) compare a lecture and a discussion?
     (*Discussion* is the last content word in the new information.)

                                    ●

B: (I) think (a lecture)'s more formal than (a discussion).
     (*Formal* is the last content word in the new information.)

NOTE: The new information does not have to be in a continuous string of words.

Example 2:

Today's topic is carbohydrates. We'll start with the molecular structure of carbohydrates.

                            ●   ●

Today's topic is carbohydrates. (We)'ll start with the molecular structure of (carbohydrates).

Situation 1. A question in a lab

A: What color should our chemical solution be?

B: Blue | —dark blue.

Situation 2. Two colleagues discussing a journal article

A: Did you read Professor Bond's paper?

B: I tried, | but it was too complicated.

A: Her papers are always complicated. Did you read her first paper? It was nearly impossible!

B: I know. It took me forever.

Situation 3. Two administrators discussing candidates for a job

A: I'm going to interview Clark and Perkins. Do you know them?

B: Yes. I met them at a conference in July.

A: What do you think of them?

B: I think Clark's more experienced than Perkins. But they're both good | —
really good.

Situation 4. A discussion about music

A: How would you compare Beethoven and Brahms?

B: Brahms is more romantic than Beethoven.

Situation 5. In a bookstore

A: I'm looking for a textbook on physiology. I found some new textbooks, |
but do you have any used ones?

B: I don't think so. We've already sold the used ones.

Situation 6. Two friends talking about work

A: My company is sending me to Albania to do some research.

B: That sounds fascinating. What part of Albania?

A: Tirana. It's the capital. But if I had a map, | I'm not even sure I could find
Albania.

B: It's on the Adriatic, | kind of between Yugoslavia and Greece.

A: Isn't it communist?

B: It used to be communist. Now it's a democracy | —or at least trying to be-
come a democracy.

Situation 7. Two colleagues talking

A: I'm looking for a speaker for our next seminar. Do you have any ideas?

B: What kind of speaker?

A: I'd like to find someone to talk about computer ethics.

B: What aspect of computer ethics?

A: Privacy on the Internet.

B: How about Jane Foster?

A: She might be OK, | but I really want someone dynamic.

B: Nancy Park's dynamic. But I wonder if she's available.

A: She's never available. Her schedule's always too full.

Passage 1

For next week's project, | you'll need the computer. If you've never

used the computer, | you'll have to attend a special seminar.

Passage 2

A morpheme is the basic unit of meaning in a language. There are two

major types of morphemes. First, let's look at free morphemes. "Group"

is a free morpheme. "Child" is also a free morpheme. So free morphemes

are independent words.

Passage 3

The Italian Renaissance began in the late thirteenth century, | and it did

not end until the fifteenth century. Florence was the center of the Renais-

sance.

☞ **EXERCISE 5.**   Listen to your instructor read this dialog. Mark the primary stress according to what you hear.

A: What was your major?

B: Organic chemistry.

A: Really? Mine was inorganic chemistry.

> Sometimes new information is contained in a part of a word. In these cases, primary stress shifts to the syllable containing the new information.

☞ **EXERCISE 6.**   In the following dialogs,
                      a. Underline the new information.
                      b. Put parentheses around old information.
                      c. Mark the primary stress on the new information.
                      d. Read each passage aloud.

Example:

   A: What's our dependent variable?
   B: Subjects' performance on the TOEFL.
   A: Good. What's our independent variable?
   B: The amount of time they've been in the United States.

                              ●
   A: <u>What's</u> (our) <u>dependent variable</u>?

                              ●
   B: <u>Subjects' performance on the TOEFL</u>.

                  ●   ●
   A: <u>Good</u>. (What's our) <u>in</u>(dependent variable)?

                                              ●
   B: <u>The amount of time</u> (they)<u>'ve been in the United States</u>.

Situation 1. Two colleagues discussing a third colleague's work

   A: I heard that Max is writing a new book. What's the topic?

   B: Microbiology.

   A: Is this his first book?

   B: Actually, | he also wrote one on psychobiology.

Situation 2. Two colleagues discussing their research results

   A: Look. I think we have a bimodal distribution. There are seven scores of 40 and seven scores of 54.

   B: Actually, | it's unimodal. The score of 58 appears nine times.

Situation 3. Two colleagues working on a math formula

   A: So next let's calculate d^2 (*d* squared).

   B: No, | first we need r^2 (*r* squared).

☛ **EXERCISE 7.**   Listen to the following dialog. Mark the primary stress according to what you hear.

Situation. A group discussion

   A: So in your opinion, | which *interest rate would be most advantageous?

   B: The higher rate.

   A: The higher rate. That's right.

When A says, "The higher rate," the speaker is repeating precisely a message unit from B. In A's repetition, the primary stress echoes the stress of the original message unit.

Notice that no new information is conveyed when A repeats it, but the repetition itself does have a new role in the conversation—to convey one or more of the following.

---

*compound noun

- A understood the answer;
- A is affirming the answer;
- A wants the rest of the group to be sure to catch it.

In some situations, such as in a classroom or other large-group contexts, we need to repeat someone's comment or response to a question. When you do so, be sure to place primary stress on the same word as in the original message unit.

☞ **EXERCISE 8.**   In the following dialogs,
   a. Mark the primary stress.
   b. Read each passage aloud.

Situation 1. A group discussing architecture

A: Who knows who designed the Falling Water House in Pennsylvania?

B: Frank Lloyd Wright.

A: Frank Lloyd Wright. That's right.

Situation 2. B is helping A with a paper

A: What was Kohlberg's first stage of moral reasoning? I can't remember.

B: The preconventional stage.

A: The preconventional stage. Thank you. And what was the second stage?

Situation 3. A is giving a seminar on ethics

A: Can someone give an example of an ethical dilemma?

B: Cloning sheep.

A: Cloning sheep. Good. Let's give that situation some consideration.

☞ **EXERCISE 9.**   In Your Own Words

    a. Write three short dialogs or passages reflecting the discourse from your academic or professional field. Each should contain a sentence in which the primary stress does not come on the last content word.

    b. Mark the primary stress.

    c. Read the dialogs or passages aloud with a partner.

You can use these frames to create your dialogs or passages, or you can write your own. Be creative!

A: How would you compare _____ and _____?

B: Well, _____ is (more/less) _____ than _____.

A: What kind of _____ is this?

B: It's a(n)_____ _____.

    Today let's talk about _____. There are _____ (number) types of _____. First we'll look at _____ (one type) _____.

☞ **EXERCISE 10.**   In Your Own Words

    a. If you have seen any of these movies, give your own rating.

        * = poor; ** = fair; *** = good; **** = excellent.

    b. Explain the table of movie ratings below to a partner.

    c. Monitor your use of primary stress.

Movie	Critic #1	Critic #2	Critic #3 = you!
Gone with the Wind	**	***	
The Godfather	***	**	
A Passage to India	****	***	
Field of Dreams	***	***	

☞ **EXERCISE 11.** In Your Own Words
  a. Explain the graph below to your class or a partner.
  b. Monitor your use of primary stress.

Semiannual Use of Natural Gas to Heat a Business

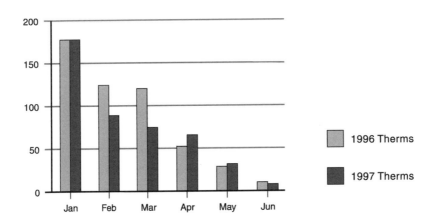

How well does the primary stress rule work?

The principle of placing primary stress on the last content word in new information is fundamental to English rhythm and melody. Because it is related to meaning, it has a significant effect on a speaker's intelligibility. Native speakers instinctively follow it, and you will hear them follow it with great regularity. It is, however, a generalization. You will undoubtedly hear native speakers appear to deviate from the rule. That is, they may put primary stress on a word other than the one you would predict.

This does not make the rule invalid, nor does it mean that the speaker is wrong. Rather, there are other possible explanations.

- A speaker's pattern may follow a variation of the rule that you have not studied yet. There are some refinements which are covered in Discourse Domains in the workbooks. In addition, there are a few other special cases that you should be aware of. *Speechcraft* will not address these cases in detail, but following are some examples.

Sometimes the last noun is stressed, instead of the last content word.

       ●   ●

What books have you read?   I've got some letters to write.

        ●   ●

Here are the tickets I bought.   There's a page missing.

Certain sentence-final time adverbials do not attract primary stress.

       ●   ●

It's time to go now.   How was the conference last week?

- A speaker's intent governs the way he or she assigns words as new or old information. That is, sometimes a speaker will choose to stress or not stress a word for some special effect. The human mind is complex, and it is difficult to account for all of these possibilities in one generalization.

Regardless, *if you follow the rule yourself, you will always make an accurate prediction.* The rule is extremely powerful and can help make your spoken messages meaningful and clear to others.

D-6

PRIMARY STRESS—NEW INFORMATION IN FUNCTION WORDS

☞ **EXERCISE 1.**   a. Listen to the following dialog.
   b. Mark the primary stress according to what you hear.

A: Did you hear? Acme Foods is going to announce a new product.

B: I hope it's not until after June. That's when we announce our new product.

A: Actually, it's going to be before June.

Primary stress goes on new information.

Old information does not receive primary stress, but is low pitch and quiet.

In a string of new information, primary stress goes on the last content word. If there is no new content word, primary stress goes on the last function word in the new information.

Function Words

prepositions
auxiliaries
pronouns (personal, relative, etc.)
negatives
all forms of the verb *be*
question words
articles

In the boldface message units, notice that the new information consists only of function words, the last of which carries the primary stress.

A: This new computer just arrived for Mr. Kramer. I didn't know he was getting another one.

●

B: **But that's not who it's for.** It's for Judy Miller.

A: Where are the beakers? I looked in the desk.

●

B: **Look above the desk.** In the cabinet.

☞ **EXERCISE 2.**   a. Underline the new information in each message unit.
b. Put parentheses around the old information.
c. Mark the primary stress.
d. Then read the dialogs aloud with a partner.

Examples:

●

A: (This) <u>new computer just arrived for Mr. Kramer</u>. (I) <u>didn't know</u> (he) <u>was</u>

●

<u>getting another</u> (one).

●   ●

B: <u>But</u> (that)<u>'s not who</u> (it's) <u>for</u>. (It's for) <u>Judy Miller</u>.

●   ●

A: <u>Where are the beakers</u>? (I) <u>looked in the desk</u>.

●   ●

B: (Look) <u>above</u> (the desk). (In) <u>the cabinet</u>.

Situation 1. Two friends leaving from work

A: I hope you'll give me a call. I need to talk to you about my data.

B: I will if I can. But I'm really busy.

Situation 2. Two colleagues talking

A: I just finished reading a terrific article.

B: What was it on?

A: Educational policy in the nineteenth century.

Situation 3. Two colleagues trying to get together

A: Do you still want to get together tomorrow at 9:00?

B: Sure. How about at Espresso Royale? That's where I'll be.

Situation 4. A has a meeting in B's office

A: I need to get to your office. Isn't it in Lincoln Hall?

B: No. But it's near Lincoln Hall. It's in the *Science Building.

Situation 5. An English pronunciation class

A: So, when we want to find the stress of a word, | we should find the key syllable, | then determine the rule?

B: No. You find the key syllable after you determine the rule.

Situation 6. A job interview

A: We need someone who can speak either Spanish or French.

B: I can speak Spanish and French!

☛ **EXERCISE 3.**   a. Listen to the following dialog.
                       b. Mark the primary stress according to what you hear.

A: How are you?

B: I'm fine. How are you?

> NOTE 1: Pronouns (and other proforms like *one, anyone, some, someone, anything, something, there, here,* and *then*) substitute for known information. It is usually clear from the speech situation that pronouns refer to shared—and therefore "old"—information. In A's part, *How* and *are* are new information—and function words. We place stress on the last function word in new information.

●

A: How are (you)?

---

*compound noun

NOTE 2: However, pronouns can attract attention as new information. In the dialog above, Speaker B uses *you*. In the context of the dialog, the meaning of the word *you* has changed; it now refers to a different person: Speaker A. *You* is new information; its new content attracts primary stress.

●

B: I'm fine. (How are) you?

If there is no new content word, primary stress goes on the last function word in new information. However, proforms do receive stress when they are given new meaning.

☞ **EXERCISE 4.**   Read these examples aloud.

Situation 1. Two colleagues talking

●

A: That new *computer lab is so nice! Have (you) been in (it)?
B: Not yet!

Situation 2. Two colleagues talking

●

A: I waited fifteen minutes for you. Where were (you)?

●

B: I was in the lab. (Where were) you?
A: I was just across the hall!

Situation 3. Two colleagues in their office

●   ●

A: When they're done fixing the computer, (they're) supposed to call (me).

●   ●

B: Really? According to Joe, | (they were supposed to call) me.

---

*compound noun

☞ **EXERCISE 5.**   a. Underline the new information in each message unit.
                    b. Put parentheses around the old information.
                    c. Mark the primary stress.
                    d. Then read the dialogs aloud with a partner.

Situation 1. Two colleagues talking

A: The committee just made their *promotion decisions.

B: How do you know? Are you on it?

A: No, | but I heard about it | from someone who is.

Situation 2. Two colleagues talking

A: I missed the last *staff meeting.

B: You should have been there. There was a big argument.

Situation 3. Two colleagues working on a report

A: I couldn't find any recent articles on the economy of Ghana.

B: But there are some. Look in the *Commerce Library.

Situation 4. Two colleagues in their office

A: There's a fax for you. It's on the desk.

B: It must be for you. It has your name on it.

Situation 5. Two colleagues in the computer lab

A: I just tried to send a message on *e-mail, | but I couldn't. I can't even access my account.

B: You can send it on my account | if you want.

---

*compound noun

☞ **EXERCISE 6.**   Before or After?

a. Your partner will read a pair of names.

●   ●

b. Say, "A lived before B" or "A lived after B." Take turns reading the names and responding.

c. Then think of other pairs of famous people and ask another partner about them.

1. Sir Isaac Newton and Indira Ghandi
2. Margaret Thatcher and Ghengis Khan
3. Confucius and Michelangelo
4. Catherine the Great and Francisco Franco
5. Martin Luther King, Jr., and Shakespeare
6. Marco Polo and Jacqueline Kennedy Onassis

☞ **EXERCISE 7.**   Questions and Answers

a. Ask a partner about the following topics.

b. Monitor your use of primary stress.

Example:

●

A: Do you have a computer?

●   ●

B: Yes, I do. Do you have one?

●

A: No, I don't.

"Do you . . . ?"	"Have you (ever) . . . ?"
. . . like chemistry	. . . seen *Casablanca*
. . . speak Korean	. . . published an article
. . . bring your lunch to work	. . . climbed a mountain
. . . listen to classical music	. . . visited Saudi Arabia
. . . write in a journal	. . . gone skiing

D-7

INTONATION

In Groundwork, we used a pitch **jump** to illustrate the three intonations—fall, rise, and fall-rise. They created these patterns.

☛ **EXERCISE 1.**   Listen to the following dialog containing pitch jumps. For each message unit, circle the intonation: ↓ for a fall, ↑ for a rise, and ↳ for a fall-rise.

	Fall	Rise	Fall-Rise
● A: What's the matter?	↓	↑	↳
● B: Too much work.	↓	↑	↳
● A: Take a break.	↓	↑	↳
● B: I should |	↓	↑	↳
● but I'll have to wait.	↓	↑	↳
● A: You can't spare five minutes?	↓	↑	↳
● B: I guess so.	↓	↑	↳
● A: Good.	↓	↑	↳
● Do you want to talk, |	↓	↑	↳

or just watch TV?   ↓   ↑   ↳

B: Let's talk.   ↓   ↑   ↳

> Two important pitch changes in the melody of English speech consist of
>
> - pitch move on the primary stress and
> - intonation—the direction of the pitch after the pitch move.
>
> Intonation helps mark the end of a message unit and can signal certain kinds of meaning.

Intonation with Pitch Jump Patterns

The three melody patterns in Exercise 1 share the same pitch move—a pitch jump. But after the pitch jump the intonation moves toward a different part of the voice range in each pattern.

In the first pattern below, the intonation makes a long fall, ending in the low part of the voice range. In the second pattern, the intonation makes an additional rise to the high part of the voice range. And in the last pattern, the intonation makes a fall-rise that goes low, then rises to the middle part of the voice range.

Low Range   High Range   Rise-to-Mid Range

These three patterns convey distinct meanings when combined with different grammatical structures. Meanings will be discussed in the next sections. First, however, you should be aware that native speakers of English use jump patterns as only one way to convey the meanings; another common way is to use drop patterns.

Intonation with Pitch Drop Patterns

In the first pattern below, the voice drops at the primary stress, then stays down at the low part of the voice range and fades out. In the second pattern, the long rise takes the voice up from the pitch drop into the high range. In the last pattern, the intonation rises from the pitch drop toward the mid range.

Low Range   High Range   Rise-to-Mid Range

You can use either the jump version or the drop version—whichever is more comfortable for you—whenever you need a low-range pattern, a high-range pattern, or a rise-to-mid-range pattern. In every conversation, native speakers mix the jump and drop versions for all three patterns.

The Meaning of the Low-Range Patterns

The basic meaning of the low-range patterns is assertive and final. The speaker is conveying conviction and completion.

You can use either the jump version or the drop version for simple **statements** and **commands.**

Pitch Jump   Pitch Drop

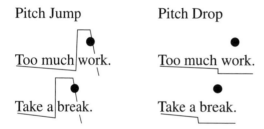

Too much work.   Too much work.

Take a break.   Take a break.

You will also see other uses for the low-range patterns in the Discourse Domains sections in the workbooks. These uses include information questions, narrowed questions, and the last message unit in a series or a set of choices.

☛ **EXERCISE 2.**   Practicing the Low-Range Patterns
                      a. Read the following dialogs aloud.
                      b. Use a pitch jump or a pitch drop.

Situation 1. Two colleagues talking

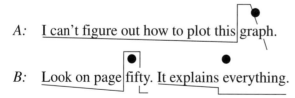

A: I can't figure out how to plot this graph.

B: Look on page fifty. It explains everything.

Situation 2. Two colleagues meet on the street

A: I want to tell you what happened today at the office. Our supervisor is crazy!

       You won't believe it.

B: I'm headed for the library. Tell me about it on the way.

Situation 3. Two roommates talking

●   ●

A: I'll see you later. I'm going to a lecture.

          ●   ●

B: It's so early in the morning! It must be important.

    ●   ●

A: It is. It's on some new research in dialectology.

     ●   ●

B: Take notes! You can tell me about it later.

> NOTE 1: Study the lines of the falling intonation with the pitch jump.

When the pitch jump occurs on the last syllable (e.g., *way*), the pitch of the falling intonation **slides** down. When the pitch jump does not occur on the last syllable (e.g., *crazy*), the pitch of the falling intonation **steps** down onto the next syllable after the pitch jump.

The Meaning of the High-Range Patterns

When a high-range pattern is used, the speaker wants to make sure that the utterance is understood as a question, especially when grammar alone does not signal a question. For example, a high-range pattern (either the jump or drop version) is used for **statement questions,** since the grammatical structure does not signal a question.

Pitch Jump   Pitch Drop

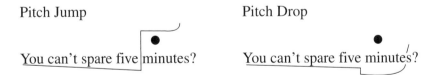

You will also see other uses for the high-range patterns in the Discourse Domains sections in the workbooks. These uses include *yes/no* questions and repetition questions. You will see, however, that the high-range patterns are not the only possible patterns for these two structures.

☞ **EXERCISE 3.**   Practicing the High-Range Patterns
a. Read the following dialogs aloud.
b. Use a high-range pattern—jump or drop—on the statement questions.

Situation 1. Two scientists talking

A: Let's go use the oscilloscope down in the lab.

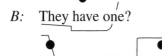

B: They have one?

A: Sure! You didn't know that?

Situation 2. Two colleagues working on their computers

A: Be careful! I heard there's a new *computer virus.

B: You didn't hear it was a hoax?

A: No kidding! You're sure?

B: Yes!

Situation 3. Two colleagues working on an important deadline

A: You didn't get any sleep?

B: I look that bad?

A: You want the truth?

---

*compound noun

The Meaning of the Rise-to-Mid-Range Patterns

The rise-to-mid-range patterns signal that the utterance is incomplete or that there is some hesitation or uncertainty about what is being said. Again, you can use either the jump version or the drop version.

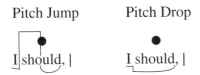

Pitch Jump   Pitch Drop

I should, | I should, |

The rise-to-mid-range patterns are used primarily in the following situations.

Nonfinal phrases: I should, |

Nonfinal elements in a series: The class meets Mondays, | Tuesdays, | [and Fridays.]

Notice that the jump and drop patterns can be mixed in the same sentence. "Fridays" would have a low-range pattern as the last element in the series.

As you will see in the Discourse Domains sections in the workbooks, the rise-to-mid-range patterns are also used with nonfinal elements in choice questions.

☛ **EXERCISE 4.**   Practicing the Rise-to-Mid-Range Patterns
   a. Read the following dialogs aloud.
   b. Use a rise-to-mid-range pattern—jump or drop—on the message units that are nonfinal.

Situation 1. Two colleagues talking

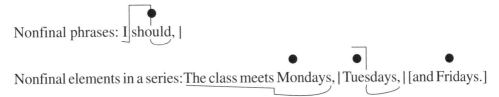

A: If you're not busy, | I'd like you to translate this.

B: Let me shut down the computer, | then I can take a look.

Situation 2. Two colleagues planning their schedules

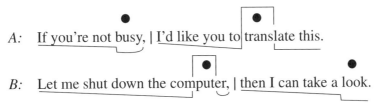

A: If I can fit it into my schedule, | I'm going to take Japanese.

B: They have openings in the sections at ten, | twelve, | and three.

A: If there's a class at four, | it would be more convenient.

B: Let me check.

Situation 3. A colleague (B) getting some advice from another colleague (A) about an oral presentation

A: When you present your paper, | just be sure to speak slowly, | clearly, | and

loudly.

B: I'll try, | but I'm just afraid they won't understand me.

A: If you practice it, | I think you'll feel a lot more comfortable.

NOTE 2: The drop version of the rise-to-mid-range pattern is also used for addressing the person you are speaking to. This applies when the name precedes your statement or question.

Example: Andrew, | could you help me set up my *database?

Example: Elizabeth, | I liked your *Web page.

You should be aware that the jump version of the rise-to-mid-range pattern is used for addressing children but not adults. Furthermore, the low-range pattern would sound inappropriately harsh for this purpose.

---

*compound noun

Summary

Categories of Melody Patterns and Their Meanings			
	Low Range Complete, Assertive	**High Range** Special Question	**Rise-to-Mid Range** Incomplete or Hesitant
Pitch jump and intonation			
Pitch drop and intonation			

☞ **EXERCISE 5.**   Practicing Intonation Patterns
a. Circle L for low range, H for high range, or M for rise-to-mid range.
b. Briefly tell why you selected that range.
c. Read the dialogs aloud.

Example: An instructor (A) and students in class

A: After you finish the
      assignment, | L   H   (M)   Reason: _Nonfinal message unit_

      check your answers in the book. (L) H   M   Reason: _Command_

B: And it's due next week?   L   (H) M   Reason: _Statement Question_

A: It's due on Friday.   (L) H   M   Reason: _Statement_

C: You can't give us an extension? L (H) M   Reason: _Statement Question_

A: I'd like to, | L   H   (M)   Reason: _Nonfinal message unit_

      but Friday's the deadline.   (L) H   M   Reason: _Statement_

Situation 1. Two colleagues looking at a graph

A: I'm confused about the *x*-axis.   L   H   M   Reason: _____

      It doesn't represent the
      frequencies?   L   H   M   Reason: _____

B: It represents the scores.   L   H   M   Reason: _____

A: You're sure?	L	H	M	Reason: _____
B: If I'm not mistaken,		L	H	M	Reason: _____
that's how it always is.	L	H	M	Reason: _____

Situation 2. Two friends talking

A: Remind me about who the Three Graces were.	L	H	M	Reason: _____
B: You're reading mythology?	L	H	M	Reason: _____
A: You're surprised?	L	H	M	Reason: _____
B: A little.	L	H	M	Reason: _____
The Three Graces were Thalia,		L	H	M	Reason: _____
Euphrosyne,		L	H	M	Reason: _____
and Aglaia.	L	H	M	Reason: _____

☛ **EXERCISE 6.**   Listening for Intonation Patterns
a. Write down one message unit you hear for each intonation pattern.
b. Read the sentences aloud yourself.

Low-range patterns: _____

_____

_____

High-range patterns: _____

_____

_____

Rise-to-mid-range patterns: _____

_____

_____

☞ **EXERCISE 7.**   Practicing Melody and Intonation

      a. Write two dialogs, each containing at least two terms from your academic or professional field.

      b. Use a low-range, high-range, and rise-to-mid-range pattern at least once.
- After each message unit, write L for low range, H for high range, or M for rise-to-mid range.
- Briefly tell why you selected that intonation pattern.
- Read the dialogs aloud.

Example 1:   A physics class

A: We'd like you to tell us what to emphasize (M) | when we study for the *midterm exam. (L)

B: You should look over centrifugal force, (M) | chain reactions, (M) | and magnetic inclination. (L)

A: And it's multiple choice? (H)

B: That's right, (M) | but you'll still have to show your calculations. (L)

Example 2:   Finance

A: So you think the company's problem is with the managers? (H)

B: Yes. (L)

A: There's no other explanation? (H)

B: Well, according to the consultants, (M) | it's a problem with their organizational culture. (L)

---

*compound noun

☛ **EXERCISE 8.** Practicing Melody and Intonation in Role Plays
a. Select one of the following situations to role-play with a partner.
b. The role play should contain at least one key sentence for each of the three structures indicated.
c. Write down the key sentences and practice them aloud, focusing on the melody.
d. Practice the entire role play with your partner, incorporating the key sentences into the rest of your exchange.

Situation 1.   Include a series, a command, and a nonfinal phrase.

Supervisor: It's noon, and you are preparing for a staff meeting later today. You suddenly realize that you need a summary of your proposed budget, and it is not done. You select a reliable and efficient employee to prepare the summary. Ask him or her to do it by 3:00 P.M.

Employee: You have been busy all morning fixing your supervisor's computer. Now it's noon, and you haven't gotten any of your own work done. In addition, you have to attend two important committee meetings this afternoon. You do not have time to prepare your supervisor's budget proposal.

Situation 2.   Include a statement question, a statement, and an address (e.g., "Andrew" or "Elizabeth").

Office Mate 1:   You are very busy on the computer with an important project that is due tomorrow. You share the computer with your office mate, but you are going to need it all day. Try to convince your office mate to wait until you are done with your project.

Office Mate 2:   Your office mate dominates the computer. Most of the time you don't need it anyway, but today you need to finish a report, and this is the only computer with the graphics capabilities you need. Try to convince your office mate to let you use the computer right away.

WORD LEVEL TOPICS

As Groundwork shows, word rhythm makes important contributions to discourse rhythm. In Word Level Topics, students learn patterns that will help them identify the syllable containing the major stress in polysyllabic words. In their workbooks, they will also apply these patterns to academic or professional terminology in their own fields of study and practice polysyllabic words in dialogs and passages.

WORD FOUNDATIONS

In Word Foundations, students begin the steps toward identifying the major stress of polysyllabic words: exploring word endings and finding the key and left syllables in words. The following topics are covered in Word Foundations.

WORD STRESS RULES: GETTING STARTED

In Groundwork, we saw that the rhythm of polysyllabic words consists of alternations and major stress. In order for you to be able to accurately pronounce these words you must put the major stress on the correct syllable.

Speechcraft presents four rules for finding the major stress of over twenty-five thousand polysyllabic words in English. Word Stress Domains will give you more specific information, practice opportunities, and the exceptions for each rule.

What words belong to each stress rule?

It mostly depends on the word's ending. In set 1 and set 2, as you read across each line, the stress shifts. But also notice that words that share the same ending share the same stress pattern.

Set 1:	technólogy	technícian	technológical
	musicólogy	musícian	músical
Set 2:	nécessary	necessitátion	necéssitate
	líterary	alliterátion	líterate

Neutral and basic endings, however, do not affect the stress of a word. You will learn to identify these endings in Word Foundations W-2.

Word endings help us to predict word stress regularities.

Sometimes you also need to know the part of speech or how many syllables a word contains before the ending.

Where is the stress?

Words in the categories in *Speechcraft* are stressed either on the key syllable or the left syllable, depending on the rule.

You will learn how to find the key and the left syllables in Word Foundations

W-4. In the four-part box below, the key syllable is underlined, and the left syllable is just to the left of the key.

> Nearly all the words in English are stressed either on the **key syllable** or the **left syllable.** In *Speechcraft,* you will study the stress of about twenty-five thousand words.

Key Stress Rule		V/VC Stress Rule	
Words:	*-ia-* . . . , *-io-* . . . , *-iu-* . . . , *-ien*C . . . These endings may have other endings added on: *-er, -able, -ize, -alist,* etc.	Words:	*-al, -ous* (Adj.) words ending in *-ic* *-ant, -ance, -ancy* (N., Adj.) *-ent, -ence, -ency* (N., Adj.)
Rule:	Stress the key syllable.	Rule:	Stress the left syllable when the key is spelled V or VC. Otherwise, stress the key syllable.
Examples:	*remédial, invéntion, génius, convénience, execútioner, fáshionable, famíliarize, rátionalist*	Examples:	*residual, disástrous, magnétic, contínuant, tólerance, redúndancy, detérrent, emérgence, cómpetency*
Left Stress Rule		Prefix Stress Rule	
Words:	long nouns ending in *-y, -acy* long *-fy* and *-ate* words	Words:	*-ary, -ery, -ory* *-ive, -ure* *-ative, -atory, -ature*
Rule:	Stress the left syllable.	Rule:	Stress the left syllable unless it contains a prefix. Otherwise, stress the key syllable.
Examples:	*índustry, líteracy, vérify, gráduate*	Examples:	*inquísitive, refínery, cátegory, apprehénsive, fúrniture, commúnicative, obsérvatory, líterature*

Remember, V = any vowel letter; C = any consonant letter.

To summarize, by learning to recognize some word endings and to apply a few simple rules, you will be able to correctly stress many thousands of polysyllabic words, including those you use in your academic or professional context. And you will be able to do this on your own without help. The rest of Word Foundations will give you the concepts and skills you need to use the rules effectively.

W-2

NEUTRAL AND BASIC ENDINGS

PATTERNS

☞ **EXERCISE 1.**   Read the following sentences aloud.

Set 1

Deer resíde in the woods.
Mark resídes in Boston.
Harmony resíded in the court.
She's resíding in France for the present.

Set 2

Sara is a résident of Chicago.
It's a residéntial community.
There was a small resídual effect.
He changed his place of résidence.

Many different kinds of endings can attach to words. Some endings, like the ones attached to *reside* in set 1 *(-s, -ed, -ing)*, do not affect the major stress of a word. By contrast, other endings *(-ent, -ial, -al, -ence)*, like those in set 2, can cause the major stress of a word to shift to a different syllable. Cases like those in set 2 will be discussed in later sections.

Neutral Endings and Basic Endings

In Set 1, *reside* is followed by *-s, -ed,* and *-ing*. These are examples of two important categories of endings in English: neutral endings and basic endings. They are important because of the following.

1. Neutral and basic endings are everywhere!
2. Neutral and basic endings carry important grammatical information.
3. Neutral and basic endings are often omitted or mispronounced in speech by nonnative speakers, creating the potential for misunderstanding.
4. Neutral and basic endings can attach to other kinds of endings we will be learning.
5. Neutral endings do not affect the stress of a word. That is, unlike other endings, these never cause the major stress to shift. In fact, they are irrelevant to word stress predictions we will make.
6. Basic endings also do not affect the stress of a word. However, they do help us make other kinds of predictions about how a word sounds.

Neutral Endings

All neutral endings begin with a consonant letter. You will learn three neutral endings: *-s, -'s, -ly.*

Neutral Endings
-s, -'s, -ly

Examples: *he elevate s, the lecturer 's, rapid ly.*

1. The *-s* is a neutral ending only

   - on plural nouns, e.g., *languages, institutions, exams;*
   - on third person singular present tense verbs, e.g., *determines, studies, predicts;* and
   - on fields of study that end in *ics,* e.g., *electronics, physics, economics.*

   Therefore words with final *ss, is, os, ous, us* have no neutral *-s* ending. For example, *hiss, innocuous,* and *us* have no neutral endings.
   Exceptions: the verbs *is, was,* and *has* have no neutral *-s* endings.
2. The *-'s* can be the genitive or a contraction for *is* or *has.*
3. The *-ly* ending must be part of an adjective or an adverb. For example, *to tally* and *a filly* have no neutral *-ly* endings.

Basic Endings

Basic endings begin with a vowel letter. You will learn three basic endings: *-e, -ed,* and *-ing.*

Basic Endings
-e, -ed, -ing

Examples: *to denot e, consol ed, entertain ing*

1. Basic endings come at the end of a word or immediately preceding a neutral ending.
   Most words have only one basic ending. For example, *unhinged* has only one basic ending: *-ed.*
   A neutral ending cannot come before a basic ending. For example, in *disease* there is no neutral *-s* ending.
2. The basic ending *-ed* only appears on past tense verbs or on adjectives. For example, *to seed* does not have a basic ending.

Similarly, the basic ending -*ing* only appears on present participles (e.g., *is running*) or on nouns made from -*ing* verbs (e.g., *a wedding*). This means that *to sing* does not have a basic ending.

3. Every final -*e* is a basic ending. For example, *to(e* and *tre(e*. However, final -*e* is not an ending when it's the only vowel letter in the word; for example, *the, be,* and *me* do not have a basic ending.

☞ **EXERCISE 2.** Mark all neutral and basic endings on the following words.

a. Work from the end of each word: *greetings* ←.
b. Cross off any neutral ending using a strike-out mark (/): *greetings̸*.
c. Use an open parenthesis to separate a basic ending: *greet(ings̸*.
d. If there is no neutral or basic ending, do not mark the word: *obvious*.

Remember: A word can have a neutral **and** a basic ending, e.g., *creat(es̸*.

Examples: neutral end(ings̸ a hypothesis quick̸ly disappear(ed

1. appreciates	9. was including	17. simultaneous
2. measuring instruments	10. homogeneous group	18. exceedingly
3. several occasions	11. the judge's decision	19. the antonyms
4. bring the fee	12. to rally	20. to discuss
5. decidedly	13. He will succeed.	21. It annoyed us.
6. costly decisions	14. studied biophysics	22. impinged on it
7. critically injured	15. to heed the advice	23. stress rules
8. his colleagues	16. respectively	24. It's ringing.

NOTE: You should be aware that there are other neutral endings in English. They all begin with consonant letters, and they usually attach to independent words. The following neutral endings are examples for your information. They will not be used in the rest of the textbook.

Neutral Ending	Example Word	Neutral Ending	Example Word
-*ness*	forgiveness	-*like*	businesslike
-*ful*	sorrowful	-*ward*	heavenward
-*wise*	otherwise	-*ment*	fulfillment (but not -*ament* or -*iment;* see Word Stress Domains W-6B)

PRACTICE

☛ **EXERCISE**   a. Find neutral endings and basic endings in the dialogs and passages.
b. Mark off the endings.
c. Read the dialogs and passages aloud.

Situation 1. Two colleagues talking

A: Has the Board of Trustees reached a consensus?
B: Not yet. They still need to discuss a few details. Why?
A: I was just wondering.

Situation 2. Two colleagues talking

A: Who's your favorite author?
B: It's definitely Charles Dickens. In fact, I wrote my thesis on him.

Situation 3. A job interview

A: Do you have any experience teaching?
B: I've taught three classes: Elements of Conducting, Beginning Composition, and Brass Instruments.

Situation 4. A lecture on Costa Rica

Costa Rica's government is working on ways to save their *rain forests. They have recently developed a computer software program to chart biodiversity.

Situation 5. A lecture on animals

Foxes are mammals that are found on nearly every continent. Their tails are one of their most interesting features. Foxes use their tails to help these animals stay warm, keep their balance, and send messages.

---

*compound noun

REVIEW

	Neutral Endings	Basic Endings
	-s	*-e*
	-'s	*-ed*
	-ly	*-ing*

☛ **EXERCISE**   Mark all neutral and basic endings on the following words.
a. Work from the end of each word: *greetings* ←.
b. Cross off any neutral ending using a strike-out mark (/):
greetings.
c. Use an open parenthesis to separate a basic ending:
greet(ings.
d. If there is no neutral or basic ending, do not mark the
word: *obvious*.

1. rating systems

2. varietal wines

3. virtually ignored

4. was injuring

5. Marge's opinion

6. He will need this.

7. furious

8. fingers and toes

9. coagulates

10. bring some papers

11. her critiques

12. a ludicrous request

13. to dally

14. conclusively

15. to digress markedly

16. scored more points

W-3

THE SOUNDS OF THE -S/-'S
AND -ED ENDINGS

PATTERNS

The -s and -'s Neutral Endings

To pronounce the neutral endings -s and -'s, you have two basic choices.

1. They can be pronounced with an **extra syllable: /əz/**.
2. They can be pronounced with a **single consonant sound: /s/ or /z/**. The choice between /s/ and /z/ is not important for intelligibility.

To choose between an extra syllable and a single sound, you must look at the letters immediately before the -s or -'s.

- If -s/-'s comes after these clue letters, pronounce it with an extra syllable (/əz/).

ce	ge	s/se	z/ze	sh/she	ch/che	x/xe
faces	George's	Bess's	Roz's	Nash's	coach's	Max's
		cases	quizzes	wishes	churches	fixes

- If you do not find the clue letters before the -s/-'s, use a single sound (/s/ or /z/).

day's   sleeps   values   strikes   ties   solids   Clinton's

---

☛ **EXERCISE 1.** Choosing an Extra Syllable or a Single Sound
   a. For words that need an extra syllable for -s/-'s, write "/əz/" and circle the clue letter(s) that guided your decision.
   b. For words that need a single consonant sound, write /s-z/.
   c. Read each word or phrase aloud.

Examples: emerges   /əz/   examines   /s-z/

   1. divides   _____   3. adages   _____

   2. surveys   _____   4. figures   _____

5. Hatch's	_____	16. reports	_____
6. cubes	_____	17. Elvis's	_____
7. compresses	_____	18. strengths	_____
8. Dixon's	_____	19. graphs	_____
9. pyramids	_____	20. manages	_____
10. Lopez's	_____	21. sketches	_____
11. St. Petersburg's	_____	22. bronzes	_____
12. pushes	_____	23. the public's	_____
13. prefixes	_____	24. leads	_____
14. Bush's	_____	25. sequences	_____
15. ratios	_____	26. fox's	_____

NOTE: You probably already know that it is important to pronounce the -*s* and -'*s* neutral endings. Yet many nonnative speakers, even experienced ones, omit them. It may take special practice and concentration for you to remember these endings in speech. You can use the rules above in your covert rehearsal.

The -*ed* Basic Ending

To pronounce the -*ed* basic ending, you have two basic choices.

1. It can be pronounced with an **extra syllable:** /əd/.
2. It can be pronounced with a **single consonant sound:** /d/ or /t/. The choice between /d/ and /t/ is not important for intelligibility.

To choose between an extra syllable and a single sound, you must look at the letters immediately before the -*ed*.

- If -*ed* comes after a *t* or a *d,* pronounce it with an extra syllable (/əd/).

t + ed	*d + ed*
wanted	ended
lifted	decided

- If you do not find a *t* or a *d* before the -*ed,* use a single sound (/d/ or /t/).

    stayed   figured   confessed   laughed   theorized   pronounced

---

☛ **EXERCISE 2.**   Choosing an Extra Syllable or a Single Sound

a. For words that need an extra syllable for *-ed,* write /əd/ and circle the clue letter that guided your decision.

b. For words that need a single consonant sound, write /t-d/.

c. Read each word aloud.

Examples: inclu(d)ed   _/əd/_   examined   _/t-d/_

1. divided	_____	11. missed	_____
2. conveyed	_____	12. invited	_____
3. survived	_____	13. possessed	_____
4. reminded	_____	14. reacted	_____
5. calculated	_____	15. bonded	_____
6. pushed	_____	16. answered	_____
7. handed	_____	17. judged	_____
8. reacted	_____	18. translated	_____
9. enjoyed	_____	19. reached	_____
10. comprehended	_____	20. publicized	_____

NOTE: All verbs follow the pattern given above. However, some adjective and noun forms are different. A small group of common *-ed* adjectives and nouns are pronounced as /əd/, even though they have no preceding *t* or *d*.

blessed	cussed	jagged	ragged	wretched
crabbed	dogged	kindred	rugged	
cragged	hatred	learned	sacred	
crooked	hundred	naked	wicked	

And a few adjectives can be pronounced with /əd/ or /t-d/.

aged	beloved	forked	supposed
alleged	cursed	peaked	winged

PRACTICE

☞ **EXERCISE 1.**   The *-s* and *-'s* Neutral Endings
Read across the columns, being careful with your pronunciation of the *-s/-'s* endings. Analyze them as necessary.

teaches and learns	colleges and universities
doctors and nurses	diseases and cures
raises and lowers	rises and falls
words and phrases	notes and messages
chapters and verses	pages and lines
memorizes and repeats	parts and pieces

☞ **EXERCISE 2.**   The *-ed* Basic Ending
a. Read each phrase aloud, being careful with your pronunciation of the *-ed* endings. Analyze them as necessary.
b. Ask a partner questions. Use "Have you ever . . . ?" Then switch roles, and your partner will ask you the same questions.

attended an opera	learned Italian	invented a word
studied all night	painted a picture	wanted to teach English
arrived late to class	watched a comet	started to fall asleep in class

☞ **EXERCISE 3.**   Below is a list of what Professor Bair did on the first day of class. Read each sentence aloud, being careful with your pronunciation of the *-s/-'s* and *-ed* endings. Analyze them as necessary.

1. She visited the room beforehand to be sure where it was located.
2. She arrived early and arranged all of the desks and chairs.
3. She introduced herself to her students.
4. She listed the required texts on the board.
5. She called the roll and matched each of the students' names with their faces.
6. She explained the syllabus.
7. She described her policies on grades and attendance.
8. She assigned several pages of the textbook for next time.
9. She asked her students to write down their goals for the course and other classes they were taking.

☞ **EXERCISE 4.**   Problem Solving
a. With a partner, read the following problem aloud and come up with a solution.
b. Monitor your pronunciation of the -s/-'s endings.

Liz's house, Mitch's house, and Bob's house are green, white, and yellow but not necessarily in that order. Liz's GRE scores were lower than Mitch's but higher than Bob's. The owner of the white house got the highest GRE score, and the owner of the yellow house got the lowest GRE score. What color is each person's house?

☞ **EXERCISE 5.**   a. Observe someone else in your professional or academic setting. Write down a list of the things the person does using the past tense.
b. Read each phrase aloud, being careful with your pronunciation of the -s/-'s and -ed endings. Analyze them as necessary.

Example: (Biology) She measured the growth of the plants in millimeters. She recorded the data in two separate notebooks . . . (etc.).

REVIEW

☛ **EXERCISE 1.**   The -*s/-'s* Neutral Ending
   a. Write down up to six terms you use in your professional or academic context that could be plural, possessive, or third person singular.
   b. Add an -*s* or -*'s* neutral ending.
   c. Tell whether the ending is pronounced /əz/ or /s-z/.
   d. Read each term aloud.

                                                                    /əz/ or /s-z/

_____   _____

_____   _____

_____   _____

_____   _____

_____   _____

_____   _____

☛ **EXERCISE 2.**   The -*ed* Basic Ending
   a. Write down up to six terms from your professional or academic setting that could be in the past tense.
   b. Add an -*ed* basic ending.
   c. Tell whether the ending is pronounced /əd/ or /t-d/.
   d. Read each term aloud.

                                                                    /əd/ or /t-d/

_____   _____

_____   _____

_____   _____

_____   _____

_____   _____

_____   _____

W-4

KEY SYLLABLES
AND LEFT SYLLABLES

In Word Foundations W-1, you learned the following information about stress.

> The major stress of nearly all polysyllabic words goes on the **key syllable** or the **left syllable**.

In order to identify the key and left syllables, we must look specifically at **how they are spelled.**

1. To help us identify syllables using spelling, we say that each syllable begins with a vowel letter. It contains any following consonant letters, too.

    In these examples, the last syllable of each word is underlined.

One Syllable	Two Syllables	Three or More Syllables
gr<u>aph</u>	cred<u>it</u>	econom<u>ic</u>
l<u>ist</u>	progr<u>am</u>	paragr<u>aph</u>
st<u>op</u>	ech<u>o</u>	misinterpr<u>et</u>

2. Since a syllable begins with a vowel letter, we need to know which letters are vowel letters. Of course, *a, e, i,* and *o* are vowel letters. But as you will see later in this lesson, *u* and *y* are not always vowel letters.

Review: Characteristics of Syllables

- Syllables carry the rhythmic alternations of a word.
- Syllables have one vowel sound.
- Key and left syllables help us determine where the major stress goes.
- Key and left syllables begin with a vowel letter.

PATTERNS
Key Syllables

What is the key syllable?

1. The key syllable occurs at the end of a word or immediately to the left of an ending.
2. The key syllable consists of

    a. all adjacent vowel letters (special cases will be treated below) and
    b. any additional consonant letters up to the end of the word or up to an ending.

The key syllable is underlined in these words.

ech<u>o</u>	str<u>ict</u>	dec<u>ide</u>	cont<u>our</u>	r<u>each</u>
ech<u>o</u>ing	str<u>ict</u>ly	dec<u>ide</u>dly	cont<u>our</u>s	r<u>each</u>ed
				r<u>each</u>ing
				r<u>each</u>es

How can I find the key?

In order to find the key of any word, use this **Key Search Strategy.**

1. Work from the end of a word: *greetings* ←.
2. Use a strike-out mark (/) to mark off any neutral ending: *greetings̸*.
3. Use an open parenthesis to separate any basic ending: *greet(ings̸*.
4. Look to the left until you find all of the adjacent vowel letters: *greet(ings̸*.
5. Underline all vowel and consonant letters up to the end of a word or up to an open parenthesis or a neutral ending: *gr<u>eet</u>(ings̸*.

☞ **EXERCISE 1.**   Practice finding key syllables. Underline the key in each word below. Use the Key Search Strategy.

Examples: dr<u>ench</u>(es̸   imp<u>air</u>(ing

1. school's	5. concerns	9. proudly	13. endorsed
2. third	6. appeared	10. admires	14. stirringly
3. sound	7. promoted	11. timing	15. undaunted
4. audit	8. growing	12. enhance	16. please

<u>Vowel Sounds, Vowel Letters, and Syllables</u>

Sometimes, two vowel letters together represent one single vowel sound.

imp**ai**ring, sch**oo**ls, s**ou**nd, app**ea**red, pr**ou**dly, und**au**nted

At other times, two vowel letters together represent two separate vowel sounds—two separate syllables. This happens when the first letter is an *i* or a *u*.

dieted	fluid
bias	duet
triad	nuance

Note that *i*V and **u**V spellings represent two separate syllables.

Follow these guidelines for finding the key syllable in such words.

1. *i*V spellings (*ia, io, iu, iet, ien*C) represent two syllables and two separate vowel sounds. Therefore only the V of an *i*V spelling is in the key syllable.

   di<u>e</u>ted   bi<u>as</u>   tri<u>ad</u>

2. *u*V spellings *(ua, ue, ui, uo)* represent two syllables and two separate vowel sounds. Therefore only the V of a *u*V spelling is in the key syllable.

   flu<u>id</u>   du<u>et</u>   nu<u>an</u>ce

Key Syllable

1. The key syllable occurs at the end of a word or immediately to the left of an ending.

2. The key syllable consists of

   a. all adjacent vowel letters but only the V of *i*V and **u**V spellings and
   b. any additional consonant letters up to the end of the word or up to an ending.

☞ **EXERCISE 2.**   Practice finding key syllables. Underline the key in each word below. Use the Key Search Strategy.

Example: imp<u>air</u>(ing

1. reputedly	5. causing	9. mouse	13. laugh
2. truants	6. diodes	10. mountain	14. ruined
3. relaxing	7. needles	11. fortune	15. achieves
4. viand	8. coaxed	12. sustaining	16. pliantly

The letters y *and* u: *A vowel or a consonant?*

The letter *y* is a consonant letter at the beginning of a word. Everywhere else, it is a vowel letter. In these examples with *y* letters, the key is underlined.

y Is a Consonant Letter	*y* Is a Vowel Letter
<u>y</u>acht	st<u>y</u>le
<u>y</u>ard	sta<u>y</u>ed

The letter *u* is almost always a vowel letter. However, it is a consonant letter in the following situations.

qu spellings: *quest, unique.* After the letter *q*, *u* is a consonant letter. It is sometimes pronounced /w/ and sometimes /Ø/ (silence).

*gu*V spellings: *language, guest.* If a *u* follows a *g* and comes before a vowel (V), *u* is a consonant letter. It is sometimes pronounced /w/ and sometimes /Ø/. Notice that in *gu* spellings followed by a consonant, *u* is a vowel letter.

u Is a Consonant Letter	*u* Is a Vowel Letter
qu<u>i</u>te	g<u>u</u>m
pl<u>a</u>que	Aug<u>u</u>st
gu<u>ar</u>d	g<u>au</u>nt
distingu<u>i</u>sh	

The letter **y** is a consonant letter at the beginning of a word.

The letter **u** is a consonant letter in **qu** and **gu**V.

NOTE: See Appendix 2, section A, for patterns that predict the sound of the consonant *u*.

☛ **EXERCISE 3.**   Practice finding key syllables. Underline the key in each word below. Use the Key Search Strategy.

Example: ann<u>oy</u>(ing

1. quench	5. acquaint	9. disobeyed	13. crypt
2. rough	6. yelling	10. yearly	14. value
3. delaying	7. critique	11. anguish	15. augustly
4. gushing	8. quietly	12. guest's	16. preying

Left Syllables

What is the left syllable?

---

1. The **left syllable** comes immediately to the left of the **key syllable**.

2. The left syllable consists of

   a. a vowel letter and
   b. any additional consonant letters up to the beginning of the key syllable.

The left syllable is marked with a wavy line (‿) in these words, and the key is underlined.

dim<u>in</u>ish	strat<u>eg</u>ic	cont<u>in</u>ued	<u>un</u>ique
chall<u>eng</u>ing	ab<u>and</u>on	rev<u>is</u>ing	ang<u>uish</u>
conc<u>urr</u>ed	d<u>iet</u>	unr<u>uin</u>ed	equ<u>ipp</u>ed

How can I find the left syllable?

In order to find the left syllable of any word, use this **Left Search Strategy.**

1. Find the key: *devel<u>op</u>(ing, request*s*.*
2. Look left until you find a vowel letter: *develop*ing ←   *request*s ←.
3. Underline with a wavy line (‿) the vowel letter and all consonant letters up to the key: *devel<u>op</u>ing, request*s*.*

☛ **EXERCISE 4.**   Practice finding key and left syllables. Use the Key Search Strategy and the Left Search Strategy.
a. Underline the key syllable.
b. Put a wavy line (〰) under the left syllable if there is one.

Examples: reach(es   astound(ing

1. escaping	6. mythic	11. acquired	16. syllable
2. interested	7. beguiled	12. introduced	17. yawns
3. stress	8. promoted	13. guzzled	18. wondered
4. height	9. determine	14. guessed	19. duets
5. requires	10. greatly	15. cruelly	20. tutoring

Exceptions

1. In these nine words, the *ui* represents one vowel sound, not two.

recruit	suit	juice	bruise	biscuit
fruit	pursuit	cruise	circuit	

2. The letter *u* is a vowel (/uw/) in the following words.

ambiguity	ambiguous	argue	contiguity	contiguous

3. In the spelling pattern *sua/sue, u* is pronounced /w/. For example, *persuade, suave, suede.*
4. The letter *u* is a consonant in *build, built, buy.*
5. The letter *y* is a vowel letter in *yttrium, ytterbium, Yggdrasil, ylang-ylang.*

PRACTICE AND REVIEW

The key syllable occurs at the end of a word or immediately left of an ending. It consists of all adjacent vowel letters (but only the V of *i*V and *u*V spellings), plus any additional consonant letters.

The left syllable occurs just to the left of the key. It consists of a vowel letter, plus any additional consonant letters.

diminish   strategic   continued   dieted   requested

☞ **EXERCISE**   In the following sentences,
   a. Underline the key syllable and mark the left syllable with a wavy line (⌣⌣) in the content words.
   b. Read each sentence aloud.

1. To *cram* (for a test, interview, etc.) means to prepare intensely and quickly for a brief time before the event.
2. To *blow off* a class or meeting means to miss it on purpose.
3. "I aced it" means "I did extremely well on it."
4. To *screw up* a test or a *lab project means to ruin it—to do it wrong or not well.
5. *Cool* has been in vogue for a long time. It describes things that are fun, interesting, great, etc.
6. "It was a riot" means that it was a lot of fun, or comic.
7. If you are *stressed out,* you are upset and tense.
8. If you are *bummed out,* you are depressed or disappointed.
9. If you are *psyched,* you feel excited and well prepared.
10. If you are *wasted,* you are drunk or tired.
11. A *jerk* is a person who behaves annoyingly.
12. A *jock* is an athlete. Jocks have an image of not being smart.

---

*compound noun

WORD STRESS DOMAINS

You are now ready for *Speechcraft*'s word stress rules. These rules will help you discover the regularities in stress that underlie thousands of academic and professional English words. The Patterns (introductory) sections of Word Stress Domains W-5–W-8 are included in this textbook as shown below. For each word stress rule, Practice and Review sections are included in the workbooks. The Practice and Review sections are required components, as they will help you contextualize the words into your own discourse contexts. The workbooks also include the Construction Stress topics (W-9) in Word Stress Domains.

As you work on the words in Word Stress Domains, it will be helpful for you to follow this set of queries.

What rule applies?
Where is the key syllable?
Where is the left syllable?
Where is the stress?
Say the word again!

KEY STRESS RULE PATTERNS

W-5A. Final Key Rule Endings
-ion, -iate, -ial, etc.

PATTERNS

What words does the Key Stress Rule (KSR) apply to?

Key Stress Rule words have a key rule ending. A key rule ending has these characteristics.

1. It has one of the following series of letters.

   ia   *io*   *iu*   *ien*C (where C = any consonant letter).

   After these *i* + vowel letters other consonant or vowel letters may follow. Remember: the only *ie* key rule ending must continue with *n*C *(nc, nt).*

2. A key rule ending always has at least one syllable to the left of it. In the examples, the key rule ending is separated by an open parenthesis.

Words with Key Rule Endings		*No* **Key Rule Endings**	
mediate	premium	dial	(no syllable to the left of the *-ial*)
med(iate	prem(ium	carrier	(The only *ie* spelling allowed as a key rule ending is *ien*C.)
ratio	convenience		
rat(io	conven(ience		

Key rule endings (*ia, io, iu, ien*C) may continue with other letters, as in these two sets.

Set 1

i + vowel +

- other vowel letters, e.g., obvio**u**s
- consonant letters, e.g., obvio**u**s, radia**nt**

> ## Set 2
>
> *i* + vowel +
> (with or without extra vowel and consonant letters)
>
> • neutral endings, e.g., ratio*s,* the premium*'s,* obvious*ly*
> • basic endings, e.g., mediat*e,* mediat*ing,* mediat*ed*

☞ **EXERCISE 1.**   Getting Started
　　　　　　　　　　a. Is the word a Key Stress Rule word?
　　　　　　　　　　　• If so, write KSR by it.
　　　　　　　　　　　• If not, put a line through it: ———-.
　　　　　　　　　　b. For Key Stress Rule words only, separate the key rule
　　　　　　　　　　　ending with an open parenthesis.

Examples: ~~rallied~~ _____   evict(ion   _KSR_

1. bacteria	_____	14. arteries _____
2. patriot	_____	15. appreciating _____
3. steroids	_____	16. contaminate _____
4. experiential	_____	17. triumphs _____
5. lion	_____	18. deviantly _____
6. immediately	_____	19. salience _____
7. rioting	_____	20. pliant _____
8. patiently	_____	21. surliest _____
9. terrain	_____	22. fallaciously _____
10. geniuses	_____	23. chandelier _____
11. mentioned	_____	24. phial _____
12. ancient	_____	25. consortium _____
13. defied	_____	26. deceived _____

Where is the key syllable?

The key is immediately to the left of the key rule ending, as underlined.

remedial	Georgian	precaution
rem<u>ed</u>(ial	G<u>eorg</u>(ian	prec<u>aut</u>(ion
convenience	invention	Acheulian
conv<u>en</u>(ience	inv<u>ent</u>(ion	Ach<u>eul</u>(ian

> REMINDER: The key syllable consists of the vowel letter or pair of vowel letters closest to the key rule ending and all following consonant letters up to the key rule ending. Remember to include in the key syllable only the V of *i*V and *u*V spellings.

*i*V Spellings	*u*V Spellings
*ia, io, iu, ien*C, *iet*	*ua, uo, ue, ui*
deviation	tuition
devi<u>at</u>(ion	tu<u>it</u>(ion

> NOTE: In Key Stress Rule words, *ea* spellings work like *i*V and *u*V spellings—only the *a* is in the key.

**   *ea* Spellings**

creation	reaction
cre<u>at</u>(ion	re<u>act</u>(ion

Where is the stress?

The Key Stress Rule assigns stress directly onto the key syllable.

Key Stress Rule

For words with key rule endings, stress the key syllable.

---

remέd(ial	Géorg(ian	precáut(ion
convén(ience	invént(ion	Achéul(ian
deviát(ion	tuít(ion	creát(ion

> NOTE: See Appendix 2, section B, for patterns predicting the sounds of stressed vowels in the key syllable.

☛ **EXERCISE 2.**   Key Stress Rule Words
   a. Separate the key rule endings with an open parenthesis.
   b. Underline the key syllable.
   c. Mark the stress.
   d. Read each word aloud.

Examples: convén(ient   evacuát(ion

		23. ulterior
1. guardians	12. epineurium	24. a deviance
2. ambitious	13. fruition	25. initially
3. expediently	14. acquisition	26. nauseation
4. sectioning	15. auctioned	27. colloquial
5. audiences	16. obsequiously	28. initiation
6. admission	17. Haitian's	29. insouciant
7. pronunciation	18. senior	30. einsteinium
8. influential	19. excruciating	31. mediating
9. quotients	20. petitioned	32. partially
10. brilliantly	21. maturation	33. vacationed
11. ideation	22. delineation	34. olympiads

NOTE 1: There is another basic ending, *-or,* that can also follow a key rule ending. For example: *médiator, gládiator,* etc.

NOTE 2: See Appendix 2, section C, for patterns predicting the sounds of consonants before key rule endings and sounds of the *i* of key rule endings.

☛ **EXERCISE 3.**   In the dialogs below,
   a. Identify Key Stress Rule words and mark their stress.
   b. Read the dialogs aloud.

Situation 1. Two colleagues talking

A: Are you going to the colloquium?

B: I don't know. I'm kind of anxious to finish this report for Georgia. What's the topic?

A: The Industrial Revolution.

Situation 2. Two colleagues talking

A: There's a new book out on psychosocial disorders.

B: Really? Who's the author?

A: Scott Williams.

B: Oh, I've heard of him. He's supposed to be a brilliant physician.

Situation 3. Two colleagues talking

A: Where'd you learn so much about intercultural communication?

B: I spent two years working in Bulgaria.

A: It must have been a fantastic experience.

B: Yes. But financially it was really tough for me.

Situation 4. Two colleagues working on a problem

A: Do you think we can use the same equation?

B: That's a good observation. Let's try it, but I think we should be cautious about it.

Situation 5. A reporter (A) talking to a factory employee (B)

A: I have some questions about the *labor union. Is there going to be a strike?

B: You'll have to talk to the chief negotiator. He's got the most recent information.

☞ **EXERCISE 4.**   Synthesizing Word Stress Rules
LSR = Left Stress Rule   KSR = Key Stress Rule
VSR = V/VC Stress Rule   PSR = Prefix Stress Rule

For each word,
a. If you haven't studied the rule, put a question mark (?) on the line.

---

*compound noun

b. If you have studied the rule,
  • Identify it: LSR, VSR, KSR, PSR.
  • Underline the key syllable.
  • Mark the major stress.
  • Read each word or phrase aloud.

Examples:	vígorous	VSR		pictórial	KSR
	to artículate	LSR		continue	?

1. exemplification	_____		13. an orientation	_____
2. exemplifying	_____		14. the auditorium	_____
3. a companion	_____		15. an audition	_____
4. some company	_____		16. auditory	_____
5. her residency	_____		17. an aviator	_____
6. residential	_____		18. aviation	_____
7. a radiator	_____		19. a family	_____
8. radiation	_____		20. familial one	_____
9. an estuary	_____		21. so familiar	_____
10. estuarial	_____		22. an objection	_____
11. Orient	_____		23. to objectify	_____
12. oriental	_____		24. an objective	_____

Exceptions and Variability

EXCEPTIONS

1. These exceptions have key rule endings stressed on the *i* of the key rule ending.

-iable	*-ial*		*-iance/iant*		*Other*
invíable	deníal	retríal	defíance	defíant	psychíatry
nonvíable	misdíal	pretríal	relíance	relíant	messíah
relíable	redíal	mistríal	complíance	complíant	
			applíance	allíance	

2. These Key Stress Rule words have only one vowel letter in the key syllable.

coáxial	coáction	reórient	Laótian	reúnion
coércion	retroáction	preémption	Croátian	Zaírian

VARIABILITY

1. All *-fiable* words have major stress on the last *i* or the left syllable.

    Examples: classifíable, identifíable, justifíable, modifíable, verifíable
                clássifiable, idéntifiable, jústifiable, módifiable, vérifiable

2. These words have major stress on the key or the first syllable.

    Examples: interséction, viviséction, subdivísion, televísion
                íntersection, vívisection, súbdivision, télevision

W-5B. Nonfinal Key Rule Endings
-ional, -iary, etc.

PATTERNS

What words does the Key Stress Rule apply to?

You learned in Word Stress Domains W-5A that words containing key rule endings are stressed by the Key Stress Rule. You also learned that key rule endings can be followed by basic endings (e.g., condition*ing*) and Neutral Endings (e.g., radio*s*).

   The key stress rule also stresses words that have nonbasic endings following a key rule ending. Two sets of nonbasic endings are presented first. Three other sets will be introduced later in this lesson.

Nonbasic Endings following Key Rule Endings

Set 1		Set 2		
-er	*-ive*	*-al*	*-able*	*-ate*
executi**oner**	appreci**ative**	profess**ional**	fashi**onable**	disori**entate**

   Notice the *i*VC or *i*VCC key rule ending (in boldface type) immediately to the left of each nonbasic ending in sets 1 and 2.

> NOTE: Among *-al* words *-ional* is unique; in this one case only the key is left of *-ion*. The key in all other *-al* words is immediately left of *-al* (see (W-6A).

☞ **EXERCISE 1.**   Does the word have a nonbasic ending following a key rule ending?
a. If so,
   • Write out the nonbasic ending.
   • Separate the key rule ending from the stem with an open parenthesis.
b. If not, put an X on the line.

Examples:

preferential ____X____   impress(ionable __-able__

1. intersectional _____   9. combinational _____

2. exterior _____   10. passionate _____

3. commissioner _____   11. questioner _____

4. associative _____   12. periodical _____

5. unquestionable _____   13. interstitial _____

6. appropriate _____   14. requisitioner _____

7. constitutional _____   15. depreciate _____

8. enviable _____   16. unmentionable _____

Where is the key syllable?

The key is immediately to the left of the key rule ending, as underlined.

exec<u>u</u>tioner   f<u>a</u>shionable   appr<u>e</u>ciative
prof<u>e</u>ssional   dis<u>o</u>rientate

REMINDER: If an *i*V or *u*V spelling appears immediately to the left of a key rule ending, only the V of the *i*V or *u*V spelling (and all following letters up to the key rule ending) can be in the key.

_i_V Spellings   **_u_V Spellings**

ia, io, iu, ienC, iet   *ua, uo, ue, ui*
devi<u>at</u>ional   fluctu<u>at</u>ional

Remember that in Key Stress Rule words, *ea* spellings work like *i*V and *u*V spellings—only the *a* is in the key.

ea Spellings

ide<u>a</u>tional   recre<u>a</u>tional

☞ **EXERCISE 2.**   a. Separate the key rule ending with an open parenthesis.
                    b. Underline the key syllable.

Examples:
    imp<u>ass</u>(ionate   conf<u>ect</u>(ioner

1. congregational   5. initiative   9. unquestionable

2. conditioner   6. actionable   10. ideational

3. situational   7. dysfunctional   11. alleviate

4. deteriorate   8. parishioner   12. initialer

Where is the stress?

The key stress rule assigns stress directly onto the key syllable.

Key Stress Rule
For words with key rule endings, stress the key syllable.

---

execú<u>t</u>ioner   fáshionable   appréciative
proféssional   fluctuátional   dispássionate
deviátional   recreátional

NOTE: See Appendix 2, section B, for patterns predicting the sounds of stressed vowels in the key syllable, and Appendix 2, section C, for patterns predicting the sounds of consonants before key rule endings.

☞ **EXERCISE 3.** Key Stress Rule Words with Nonbasic Endings
a. Separate the key rule endings with an open parenthesis.
b. Underline the key syllable.
c. Mark the stress.
d. Read each word or phrase aloud.

Examples: excép̲t(ional   conféc̲t(ioner

1. practitioner	7. questionable	13. impressionable
2. companionable	8. vacationer	14. traditional
3. ideational	9. compassionate	15. radiative
4. unappreciative	10. situational	16. unconscionable
5. to ameliorate	11. petitioner	17. associative
6. the initiative	12. occasional	18. proportionate

Key Stress Rule	**V/VC Stress Rule**
(key rule ending plus nonbasic ending)	(not *-ional*)
traditional	maníacal
situational	zodíacal

Nonbasic Endings following Key Rule Endings

Set 3		
-y	*-ary*	*-ory*
intermé̲diary	ví̲sionary	concí̲liatory

Set 4			**Set 5**		
-ize	*-ist*	*-ism*	*-alize*	*-alist*	*-alism*
famí̲liarize	impé̲rialist	creá̲tionism	rá̲tionalize	rá̲tionalist	rá̲tionalism

☛ **EXERCISE 4.**   Does the word have a nonbasic ending after a key rule ending?

a. If so,
  - Write out the nonbasic ending.
  - Separate the key rule ending from the stem with an open parenthesis.
  - Underline the key.
  - Mark the stress.

b. If not, put an X on the line.

c. Read each key rule ending word aloud.

Examples:

parliamentary	__X__	relíg(ionist	_-ist_
1. institutionalize	_____	15. editorialize	_____
2. creationism	_____	16. allegory	_____
3. scientist	_____	17. extortionist	_____
4. judicialize	_____	18. conversationalist	_____
5. industrialization	_____	19. longevity	_____
6. brilliancy	_____	20. diversionary	_____
7. retaliatory	_____	21. specialist	_____
8. rationalist	_____	22. renunciatory	_____
9. subsidiary	_____	23. formalize	_____
10. regionalism	_____	24. journalism	_____
11. memorialize	_____	25. interventionism	_____
12. nutritionist	_____	26. reconciliatory	_____
13. stationary	_____	27. sensationalism	_____
14. nationalistic	_____	28. regionalize	_____

☛ **EXERCISE 5.** Key Rule Endings before Nonbasic Endings
a. Underline the key.
b. Mark the stress on each word below.
c. Read each word or phrase aloud.

Examples: régionalism   alléviate

1. trivialize	8. functionalism	15. professionalize
2. conversational	9. internationalize	16. Confucianism
3. deteriorate	10. a cautioner	17. actionable
4. expiatory	11. sensational	18. auxiliary
5. variative	12. recessionary	19. nationalist
6. evolutionist	13. objectionable	20. parliamentarianism
7. idiocy	14. abstractionism	21. dictionary

☛ **EXERCISE 6.** Synthesizing Word Stress Rules
LSR = Left Stress Rule   KSR = Key Stress Rule
VSR = V/VC Stress Rule   PSR = Prefix Stress Rule

For each word,
a. If you haven't studied the rule, put a question mark (?) on the line.
b. If you have studied the rule,
   • Identify it: LSR, VSR, KSR, or PSR.
   • Underline the key syllable.
   • Mark the major stress.
   • Read each word or phrase aloud.

Examples:

perfectionístic	VSR	perféctionism	KSR
so perfect	?	perféctive	PSR

1. a visionary	_____	5. illusionary	_____
2. so visual	_____	6. rather illusory	_____
3. segregated	_____	7. reconciliation	_____
4. segregationist	_____	8. reconciliatory	_____

9. to congregate   _____

10. Congregationalist   _____

11. the variability   _____

12. so variative   _____

13. an observatory   _____

14. observational   _____

15. benevolent   _____

16. a beneficiary   _____

17. expressionism   _____

18. so expressive   _____

19. by memory   _____

20. to memorialize   _____

21. memorization   _____

22. so practical   _____

23. a practicality   _____

24. a practitioner   _____

Exception

invíolable

Also, the word *behavioral* is stressed by the Key Stress Rule, although it does not have an *-ional* spelling.

V/VC STRESS RULE PATTERNS

W-6A. V/VC Rule Endings
-al, -ous, ic

PATTERNS

Which words does the V/VC Stress Rule (VSR) apply to?

The V/VC Stress Rule applies to adjectives ending in the V/VC rule endings *-al* and *-ous*.

Examples:

inaugural	triumphal	ominous	disastrous
inaugur(al	triumph(al	omin(ous	disastr(ous
cuboidal	residual	fortuitously	innocuous
cuboid(al	residu(al	fortuit(ously	innocu(ous
maniacal	periodically		
maniac(al	periodic(ally		

- Nouns with *-al* endings are **not** stressed by the V/VC Stress Rule. As you will see, the V/VC Stress Rule does not work with nouns such as the following.

  the arríval   an accrúal   a pédestal

- If the *-al* or *-ous* ending is a part of a key rule ending, use the Key Stress Rule.

  ménial   contágious
  remédial   fallácious

☛ **EXERCISE 1.**   Identifying V/VC Stress Rule Words
a. If the word is a V/VC Stress Rule word,
  • Separate off the V/VC rule ending with an open parenthesis.
  • Write VSR.
b. If it is not, put a line through it: —————.

Examples:
    the ~~arrival~~ _____   so monoton(ous   _VSR_

1. so patriarchal _____   8. atypical one _____

2. the proposal _____   9. so ambiguous _____

3. so insidious _____   10. a renewal _____

4. adventurous one _____   11. a nocturnal one _____

5. alluvial one _____   12. very obvious _____

6. oriental one _____   13. so humorous _____

7. too literal _____   14. a refusal _____

Where is the key syllable?

Use the Key Search Strategy. The key syllable is immediately to the left of the *-al* or *-ous* ending, as underlined.

ina<u>ug</u>ural	tri<u>umph</u>al	om<u>in</u>ous	dis<u>astr</u>ous
cub<u>oid</u>al	res<u>id</u>ual	fortu<u>it</u>ously	inn<u>oc</u>uous
mani<u>ac</u>al	period<u>ic</u>ally		
pharmaceut<u>ic</u>al	acoust<u>ic</u>al		

REMINDER: The key consists of all adjacent vowel letters and all following consonant letters up to the V/VC rule ending. Remember to include only the V of *i*V and *u*V spellings.

***i*V Spellings**   ***u*V Spellings**

*ia, io, iu, ien*C, *iet*   *ua, uo, ue, ui*
tri<u>umph</u>al   fortu<u>it</u>ously

Where is the left syllable?

Use the Left Search Strategy. The left syllable is immediately to the left of the key. It includes one vowel letter and any consonants up to the key.

> NOTE: Both vowels of *au, eu,* or *ou* combinations belong in the left syllable for V/VC Stress Rule words. Otherwise, only one vowel letter is in the left syllable.

inaugural	triumphal	ominous	disastrous
cuboidal	residual	fortuitously	innocuous
maniacal	periodically		
pharmaceutical	acoustical		

☞ **EXERCISE 2.**   Finding the Key and Left Syllables in V/VC Stress Rule Words
a. Separate off the V/VC Stress Rule ending with an open parenthesis.
b. Underline the key syllable.
c. Put a wavy line (‿‿) under the left syllable if there is one.

Examples: inaugur(al   ambidextr(ous

1. mystical	4. annual	7. circuitous	10. nebulous
2. neutral	5. procedural	8. clinical	11. acoustical
3. gratuitous	6. momentous	9. viral	12. contemptuous

What is the rule?

In order to use the V/VC Stress Rule, you need to evaluate the spelling of the key syllable. If it is spelled with one vowel letter (V) or a vowel letter plus a consonant letter (VC), the stress goes on the left syllable. If there is another spelling pattern in the key syllable (VV, VVC, VCC, etc.), then the stress stays on the key. If there is no left syllable, the stress goes on the key.

Whenever the stress goes on the left syllable, the key syllable is unstressed and has a reduced vowel. The alternation of stress (stressed left and unstressed key) is part of the word rhythm.

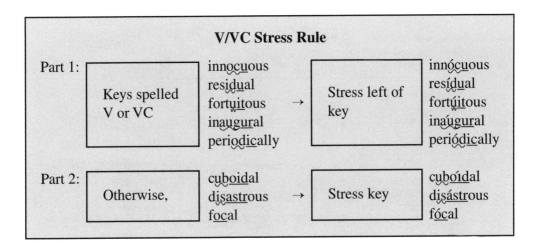

NOTE: See Appendix 2, section D, for patterns predicting the sounds of stressed vowels in left syllables. Patterns in Appendix 2, section E, predict the sounds of the underlined letters in *resídual, vírtuous, vísual, sénsuous,* and *séxual.*

☞ **EXERCISE 3.** V/VC Stress Rule Words

a. Separate off the V/VC rule ending with an open parenthesis.
b. Underline the key syllable and mark the left syllable with a wavy line (〰) in each word.
c. Circle the stress command: Key or Left.
d. Mark the major stress.
e. Read each word aloud.

Examples:

amórph(ous (Key) Left   perípher(al   Key (Left)

1. voluminous	Key	Left		11. prosperous	Key	Left
2. digitally	Key	Left		12. semiannual	Key	Left
3. overzealous	Key	Left		13. bilingual	Key	Left
4. maniacal	Key	Left		14. disloyal	Key	Left
5. cuboidal	Key	Left		15. periodontal	Key	Left
6. hypothetically	Key	Left		16. nautical	Key	Left
7. stupendous	Key	Left		17. usual	Key	Left
8. radical	Key	Left		18. periodically	Key	Left
9. factual	Key	Left		19. supplemental	Key	Left
10. conspicuous	Key	Left		20. ancestral	Key	Left

The V/VC Stress Rule also applies to adjectives and nouns with a final *ic*. Final *ic* is the key syllable, not an ending.

Examples: in económ*ic*s   photográph*ic*   magnét*ic*   the dynám*ic*s

> NOTE 1: The *ic* is also the key when a vowel letter is just to its left, e.g., *algebraic*.

> NOTE 2: A word with a basic ending after *ic* is not a V/VC Stress Rule word; e.g., *device, policed, enticing* are not stressed by the V/VC Stress Rule.

☛ **EXERCISE 4.**   V/VC Stress Rule Words
    a. Underline the key syllable and mark the left syllable with a wavy line (⌣⌣) in each word.
    b. Circle the stress command: Key or Left.
    c. Mark the major stress.
    d. Read each word aloud.

Examples:
    horréndous   (Key) Left   epidémic   Key   (Left)

1. inorganic	Key Left	10. strenuously	Key Left
2. ubiquitous	Key Left	11. mosaic	Key Left
3. electronics	Key Left	12. aeronautical	Key Left
4. biannually	Key Left	13. enormously	Key Left
5. intrinsic	Key Left	14. myopic	Key Left
6. continental	Key Left	15. rigorous	Key Left
7. miraculous	Key Left	16. Mesozoic	Key Left
8. critical	Key Left	17. dangerous	Key Left
9. enthusiastic	Key Left	18. developmental	Key Left

☞ **EXERCISE 5.**   Synthesizing Word Stress Rules
LSR = Left Stress Rule   KSR = Key Stress Rule
VSR = V/VC Stress Rule   PSR = Prefix Stress Rule

For each word,
a. If you haven't studied the rule, put a question mark (?) on the line.
b. If you have studied the rule,
  • Identify it: LSR, VSR, KSR, or PSR.
  • Underline the key syllable.
  • Mark the major stress.
  • Read each word or phrase aloud.

Examples:

electrícian	KSR	eléctric	VSR
electron	?	electrícity	LSR

1. instrumental	_____	13. technology	_____
2. instrumentation	_____	14. anonymous	_____
3. mathematics	_____	15. anonymity	_____
4. mathematician	_____	16. neutral	_____
5. morphology	_____	17. neutrality	_____
6. amorphous	_____	18. prosperity	_____
7. hallucinogenic	_____	19. prosperous	_____
8. hallucinatory	_____	20. ordinary	_____
9. hallucination	_____	21. ordinal	_____
10. technological	_____	22. ordination	_____
11. technician	_____	23. to stupefy	_____
12. technical	_____	24. stupendous	_____

Exceptions and Variability

EXCEPTIONS

1. For *-ional* words, the Key Stress Rule applies.

    excéptional   irrátional   sensátional

2. A stressed VC key

	-V*val*		-cídal, e.g.
anecdótal	infinitíval	mediéval	regicídal
	adjectíval	priméval	homicídal

3. A stressed left syllable with a VV or VCC key

míschievous	víllainous	chívalrous	lúdicrous
moúntainous	týrannous	idólatrous	házardous

4. Other

Árabic	spíritual	cátholic	pólitics (N.)
dísciplinal	ársenic (N.)	héretic (N.)	rhétoric (N.)
aríthmetic (N.)			

5. The letter *u* is a vowel in

    ambíguous   contíguous

6. The left syllable contains two vowel letters in

    treácherous   treásonous   poísonous   traítorous

VARIABILITY

These adjectives can be stressed on the key or the left syllable.

cerebral   communal   coronal   doctrinal   integral   magistral   vertebral

W-6B. V/VC Rule Endings
-V*nt*, -V*nce*, -V*ncy*

PATTERNS

Which words does the V/VC Stress Rule apply to?

The V/VC Stress Rule applies to words with these V/VC rule endings: *-ant, -ance, -ancy* and *-ent, -ence, -ency.*

Examples:

continuant	continu(ant	deterrent	deterr(ent
tolerance	toler(ance	emergence	emerg(ence
accountancy	account(ancy	competency	compet(ency
distance	dist(ance	absence	abs(ence

- These endings only apply to **nouns** and **adjectives.** Verbs with these endings, and other words ending in *-ed* and *-ing,* are **not** stressed by the V/VC Stress Rule. As you will see, the V/VC Stress Rule does not work with words such as *to comménce, to supplánt, indénted, recánting.*
- Adjectives ending in *-ent* and *-ant* can become *-ly* adverbs, also stressed by the V/VC Stress Rule: *elegantly, confidently.*
- If the *-ant, -ance, -ancy* or *-ent, -ence, -ency* is a part of a key rule ending, use the Key Stress Rule: *the brílliance, so brílliant, so convénient, her léniency.*

☛ **EXERCISE 1.**   Identifying V/VC Stress Rule Words
  a. If the word is a V/VC Stress Rule word
    - Separate off the V/VC rule ending with an open parenthesis.
    - Write VSR.
  b. If it is not a V/VC Stress Rule word, put a line through it: ————.

Examples:

~~unpatented~~   _____   refer(ences   _VSR_

1. participants   _____   5. expediency   _____

2. delinquency   _____   6. discontented   _____

3. to implant   _____   7. occupancy   _____

4. issuance   _____   8. truants   _____

9. frequency	_____	14. presence	_____
10. luxuriant	_____	15. acquaintance	_____
11. different	_____	16. ingredients	_____
12. repentant	_____	17. advocacy	_____
13. repeting	_____	18. reminiscent	_____

Where is the key syllable?

Use the Key Search Strategy. The key syllable is immediately to the left of the V/VC rule ending, as underlined.

contin<u>ua</u>nt	det<u>er</u>rent
tol<u>er</u>ance	em<u>er</u>gence
acc<u>oun</u>tancy	comp<u>et</u>ency
d<u>is</u>tance	<u>abs</u>ence

> REMINDER: The key consists of all adjacent vowel letters and all following consonant letters up to the V/VC rule ending. Remember to include only the V of *i*V and *u*V spellings.

***i*V Spellings**	***u*V Spellings**
ia, io, iu, ienC, iet	*ua, uo, ue, ui*
tri<u>um</u>phant	annu<u>it</u>ant

Where is the left syllable?

Use the Left Search Strategy. The left syllable is immediately to the left of the key.

contin̰uant	dḛterrent
to̰lerance	ḛmergence
a̰ccountancy	co̰mpetency
trḭumphant	annṵitant

What is the rule?

In order to use the V/VC Stress Rule, you need to evaluate the spelling of the key syllable. If it is spelled with one vowel letter (V) or a vowel letter plus a consonant letter (VC), the stress goes on the left syllable. If there is another spelling pattern in the key syllable (VV, VVC, VCC, etc.), then the stress stays on the key. If there is no left syllable, stress the key.

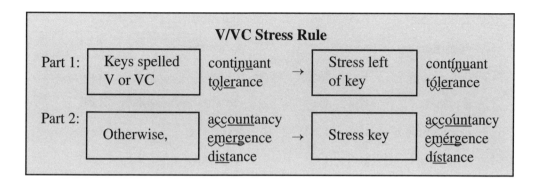

NOTE 1: Remember that *y* is a vowel letter when it follows a vowel letter, as in *clairvóyant*.

NOTE 2: The ending *-ment* is almost always a neutral ending (like *-s, -'s, -ly*). However, words spelled *-ament* and *-iment* have *-ent* V/VC endings and are stressed by the V/VC Stress Rule.

VSR	***Not* VSR**
fílament	encouragement
régiment	astonishment
impédiment	commandment

NOTE 3: See Appendix 2, section D, for patterns predicting the sounds of stressed vowels in the left syllable.

☛ **EXERCISE 2.**   V/VC Stress Rule Words
   a. Separate off the V/VC rule ending with an open paren-thesis.
   b. Underline the key syllable and mark the left syllable with a wavy line (〰) in each word.
   c. Circle the stress command: Key or Left.
   d. Mark the major stress.
   e. Read each word aloud.

Examples:
magnífic(ent	Key	(Left)	detérg(ent	(Key)	Left
1. preferences	Key	Left	5. covenant	Key	Left
2. ordinance	Key	Left	6. frequent	Key	Left
3. annoyances	Key	Left	7. president	Key	Left
4. redundancy	Key	Left	8. flamboyant	Key	Left

9. adolescent	Key	Left		18. fluctuant	Key	Left
10. constituency	Key	Left		19. performance	Key	Left
11. perpetuance	Key	Left		20. irrelevancy	Key	Left
12. a balance	Key	Left		21. violent	Key	Left
13. expectantly	Key	Left		22. reverberant	Key	Left
14. ambulance	Key	Left		23. fragrantly	Key	Left
15. resultant	Key	Left		24. compliment	Key	Left
16. extravagancies	Key	Left		25. accident	Key	Left
17. predicament	Key	Left		26. consultancy	Key	Left

☛ **EXERCISE 3.**   Synthesizing Word Stress Rules
LSR = Left Stress Rule   KSR = Key Stress Rule
VSR = V/VC Stress Rule   PSR = Prefix Stress Rule

For each word,
a. If you haven't studied the rule, put a question mark (?)
   on the line.
b. If you have studied the rule,
   • Identify it: LSR, VSR, KSR, or PSR.
   • Underline the key syllable.
   • Mark the major stress.
   • Read each word aloud.

Examples:

continuátion	_KSR_		contínuant	_VSR_
to continue	_?_		continúity	_LSR_
1. incident	_____		9. admittance	_____
2. incidental	_____		10. admissive	_____
3. lubricious	_____		11. admission	_____
4. lubricant	_____		12. residential	_____
5. lubricity	_____		13. resident	_____
6. tyranny	_____		14. residual	_____
7. tyrant	_____		15. cognitive	_____
8. tyrannical	_____		16. cognition	_____

17. cognizant	_____	21. participant	_____
18. violated	_____	22. participatory	_____
19. violation	_____	23. sacrilegious	_____
20. violent	_____	24. sacrament	_____

Exceptions and Variability

EXCEPTIONS

1. A stressed V/VC key

   -her

	allowance	complácent
adhérent	antecédent	translúcent
cohérent	impédance	interférence
inhérent	contrívance	persevérence
	oppónent	assúrance
-jac	discrépancy	endúrance
adjácent	lieuténant	pursúant
		reágent

   -par
   appárent
   transpárent

2. Stress left of VCC/VV key

		Vqu	**VCr**
círcumstance	éxcellent	cónsequent	recálcitrant
góvernance	recónnaissance	éloquent	ímmigrant
élephant	ímmigrant	súbsequent	
Prótestant	réstaurant		

3. Others

an advánce	his dissént	an accómpaniment
the ascént	the extént	intént
an evént	the descént	(mal)contént

4. Two vowels in the left syllable

    cóuntenance   tóurnament

5. Some *-ement* words that **are** stressed by the V/VC Stress Rule

    cómplement   éxcrement   récrement
    décrement   ímplement   súpplement
    élement   íncrement

VARIABILITY
These words can be stressed either on the key or left syllable.

affluent   decadent   influence
combatant   disputant   insurance
conversant   excitant   proponent
component   exponent   Renaissance
congruent

Left Stress Rule Patterns

W-7A. Left Rule Endings
-y/-i on Long Words

PATTERNS

In this lesson, you will learn the Left Stress Rule (LSR).

What words does the Left Stress Rule apply to?

1. Left Stress Rule words have a left rule ending. The first set of words we will study have *-y* and *-i* left rule endings.
2. Left Stress Rule words have at least two syllables to the left of the left rule ending: We call them "long" words. In these examples, the numbers count the syllables to the left of the *-y*.

Long (LSR)	*Not* Long

an industry
  2   1
	a quarry
	   1

the ministry
    2 1
	a treaty
	   1

a variety
  3 21
	a dairy
	   1

the methodology
    4 3 2 1
	a belly
	   1

Long words with *-y* and *-i* left rule endings are of two kinds.

• Long nouns ending in *-y* and their plurals

the ministry	the ministries
the ministr(y	the ministr(ies
the biography	the biographies
the biograph(y	the biograph(ies

- Long verbs ending in *fy* and their related forms with *fy* or *fi* + -*es*, -*ed*, or -*er*

to certify	he certifies	they certified
to certif(y	he certif(ies	they certif(ied
	she's certifying	a certifier
	she's certif(ying	a certif(ier

NOTE 1: -*ary*, -*ery*, and -*ory* are prefix endings, and -*ency* and -*ancy* are V/VC endings. None of these contains a left rule ending. -*acy* will be treated later. Study these examples.

-y Left Rule Ending (LSR)	*Not* **a -y Left Rule Ending**
acceptability	corollary
terminology	delivery
harmony	advisory
formality	frequency
loyalty	discrepancy

NOTE 2: The *f* in words like *certify, certifies* is not part of the left rule ending, but it helps identify the set of words to which the Left Stress Rule applies.

☛ **EXERCISE 1.**   Getting Started
a. If the word is a Left Stress Rule word,
- Write LSR by it.
- Separate off the left rule ending with an open parenthesis.

b. If it is not a Left Stress Rule word, put a line through it: _____.

Examples: a ~~category~~ _____   to satisf(y   _LSR_

1. his strategy _____   7. it typifies _____

2. a dolly _____   8. the apostasy _____

3. we edify _____   9. in histology _____

4. an allegory _____   10. with consistency _____

5. the booty _____   11. in the periphery _____

6. my hypocrisy _____   12. they signify _____

13. a ferry   _____   17. proximity   _____

14. two symphonies   _____   18. she implies   _____

15. the occupancy   _____   19. her anxieties   _____

16. a luminary   _____   20. a classifier   _____

Where is the key syllable?

Use the Key Search Strategy. The key syllable is immediately to the left of the left rule ending, as underlined.

the mini<u>str</u>(y   to cert<u>if</u>(y   he cert<u>if</u>(ies   they cert<u>if</u>(ied
the mini<u>str</u>(ies   she's cert<u>if</u>(ying   a cert<u>if</u>(ier

> REMINDER: The key syllable consists of all adjacent vowel letters and all following consonant letters up to the left rule ending. Remember to include only the V of *i*V and *u*V spellings.

***i*V Spellings**	***u*V Spellings**
*ia, io, iu, ien*C, *iet*	*ua, uo, ue, ui*

theo<u>log</u>(y   pauc<u>it</u>(y   vill<u>ain</u>(y   soc<u>iet</u>(y   annu<u>it</u>(y   en<u>erg</u>(y

Furthermore, only the *it* of V*ity* words is in the key.

homogene<u>it</u>(y   spontane<u>it</u>(y   the la<u>it</u>(y

Where is the left syllable?

Use the Left Search Strategy. The left syllable, marked with a wavy line (〜), is immediately to the left of the key syllable.

> NOTE: For the Left Stress Rule, the left syllable includes
>
> a. only one vowel letter or *au, eu,* or *ou* and
> b. any following consonant letters up to the key.

the͜o<u>log</u>(y   p͜au͜c<u>it</u>(y   vi͜l<u>lain</u>(y   so͜c<u>iet</u>(y   an͜nu<u>it</u>(y   ͜en<u>erg</u>(y

☞ **EXERCISE 2.**   Left Stress Rule Words: Key and Left Syllables
a. Separate off the left rule ending with an open parenthesis.
b. Underline the key syllable.
c. Put a wavy line (⌣⌣) under the left syllable if there is one.

Examples: a symphon(y   to satisf(y

1. his strategy	5. in cardiology	9. philosophy
2. with courtesy	6. some commonalities	10. in perpetuity
3. we edify	7. a classifier	11. they signify
4. your cruelty	8. heterogeneity	12. hegemony

Where is the stress?

The Left Stress Rule places stress directly onto the left syllable.

Left Stress Rule

For words with left rule endings, stress the left syllable.

---

we certif(ied   theolog(y   paucit(y   villain(y   societ(ies   annuit(y

NOTE: See Appendix 2, section D, for patterns predicting the sounds of stressed vowels in the left syllable.

☞ **EXERCISE 3.**   Left Stress Rule Words
a. Separate the left rule ending with an open parethesis.
b. Underline the key syllable and put a wavy line (⌣⌣) under the left syllable.
c. Mark the stress.
d. Read each word or phrase aloud.

Example: in realit(y

1. fortified	5. a company	9. a biography	13. his satiety
2. the liturgies	6. courtesy	10. the rivalries	14. crucified
3. a colony	7. with euphony	11. electrifying	15. the deity
4. they mollify	8. two centuries	12. she specifies	16. to clarify

☞ **EXERCISE 4.**   Left Stress Rule Words in Context
      a. Identify Left Stress Rule words.
      b. Underline the key syllable and put a wavy line ($\smile$)
        under the left syllable.
      c. Mark the stress of each word.
      d. Read each sentence aloud.

1. Analogies and metaphors can vivify a lecture and clarify unfamiliar or complex concepts.
2. Reliability and validity are two critical characteristics of experimental methodology.
3. U.S. universities are developing strategies to address the diversity of their students: gender, ethnicity, socioeconomic status, etc.
4. There has been nationwide publicity about the *language ability of international TAs and faculty.
5. Bloom's taxonomy of objectives classifies *learning behaviors into different levels of cognitive ability.

☞ **EXERCISE 5.**   Synthesizing Word Stress Rules
      LSR = Left Stress Rule   KSR = Key Stress Rule
      VSR = V/VC Stress Rule PSR = Prefix Stress Rule

      For each word,
      a. If you haven't studied the rule, put a question mark (?)
        on the line.
      b. If you have studied the rule,
        • Identify it: LSR, VSR, KSR, or PSR.
        • Underline the key syllable.
        • Mark the major stress.
        • Read each word or phrase aloud.

Examples: contínuous VSR   continúity   LSR

   continuátion KSR   to continue   ?

1. his strategies _____   5. proximal one _____

2. so strategic _____   6. in proximity _____

3. their destinies _____   7. so exemplary _____

4. approximation _____   8. they exemplify _____

*compound noun

9. We're mystified. _____   17. so admonitory   _____

10. very mysterious _____   18. his admonitions _____

11. a mystery's   _____   19. with unanimity   _____

12. so hypocritical _____   20. It's unanimous. _____

13. my hypocrisy   _____   21. an industry's   _____

14. by heredity   _____   22. industrious   _____

15. hereditary one   _____   23. with symmetry   _____

16. their destination _____   24. symmetrically   _____

Exceptions and Variability

EXCEPTIONS

There are more than two thousand words with -y/-i left rule endings. Of these, there are only a few stress exceptions. The most common are listed below.

1. Stress on the key

    an assémbly   in entreáty   a jalópy

2. Stress left of the left syllable

		-archy, e.g.	-mony, e.g.
cásualty	mélancholy	híerarchy	álimony
cítizenry	órthodoxy	pátriarchy	mátrimony
spécialty	pédagogy	óligarchy	téstimony
dífficulty	sóvereignty		céremony
épilepsy			

3. *u* is a vowel in

    ambigúity   contigúity

4. There are only three words in which VV spellings (not *i*V or *u*V) are separated into two syllables: *the peony, the poetry, to deify.* The Left Stress Rule applies to these three words.

5. There are two vowels in the left syllable of the following words: *loyalty, royalty, to speechify.*

VARIABILITY

The word *inquiry* can also be stressed on the key syllable, and *controversy* and *ignominy* can also be stressed left of the left syllable.

W-7B. Left Rule Endings
-ate, -acy

PATTERNS

What words does the Left Stress Rule apply to?

The Left Stress Rule applies to over fifteen hundred words with the following left
rule endings: *-at* + B (basic ending) *(-ate, -ated, -ating, -ator)* and *-acy (-acies)*.

To have one of these as a left rule ending, a word must pass this test: There
must be two or more syllables left of the *-at* + B or the *-acy*. For example:

Left Rule Endings	**No Left Rule Endings**

to gradu(ate
  2 1
	to misstate
	    1

indetermin(acy 4 3 2 1	racy NONE

The *-at* + B Left Rule Endings

- In these words, *-ate, -ated,* and *-ating* are left rule endings.

  to educ(ate   we educ(ated   He's educ(ating us.

- Notice that *-e, -ed,* and *-ing* are basic endings you have learned in Word
  Foundations. One more basic ending, *-or*, is common after *-at*.

  an educ(at**or**

- We can generalize the *-ate, -ated, -ating,* and *-ator* as *-at* + B.
  Another set of examples with *-at* + B left rule endings:

  to terminate   we terminated   He's terminating it.   the Terminator

☛ **EXERCISE 1.**   Construct a complete set of Left Stress Rule words by adding -*at* + B left rule endings to the stems on the left.

	-e	*-ed*	*-ing*	*-or*
Examples:				
moder-	moderate	moderated	moderating	a moderator
1. estim-				
2. gener-				
3. instig-				
4. perpetr-				

The -*acy* Left Rule Ending

In order for -*acy* to be a left rule ending, there must be at least two syllables to the left of the -*acy*. Words such as *prelacy* fail this test if we use -*acy* as a left rule ending. However, the -*y* alone is still a left rule ending (see Word Stress Domains W-7A). Therefore these words are still stressed by the Left Stress Rule.

-*acy*/-*acies* Left Rule Endings   **-*y*/-*ies* Left Rule Endings**

liter(acy   pharmac(y
legitim(acies   legac(ies

> NOTE: -*iat* + B and -*iacy* are key rule endings. Use the Key Stress Rule, **not** the Left Stress Rule: negótiating, inítiated, rádiator, immédiacy

Where is the key syllable?

Use the Key Search Strategy. The key syllable is immediately to the left of the left rule ending, as underlined.

to gradu̲ate   the perpe̲trator   indetermi̲nacy   lite̲racy
to gradu(ate   the perpetr(ator   indetermin(acy   liter(acy

Where is the left syllable?

Use the Left Search Strategy. The left syllable, marked with a wavy line (‿), is immediately to the left of the key syllable.

to gra̰du̲ate   the pḛrpe̲trator   indetḛrmi̲nacy   lḭte̲racy

---

☞ **EXERCISE 2.** Is the Word a Left Stress Rule Word?
a. If it is,
   • Write LSR for Left Stress Rule.
   • Separate off the left rule ending with an open parenthesis.
   • Identify the key syllable and left syllable.
b. If it is not, put a line through it: —————-.

Examples: to c̶r̶e̶a̶t̶e̶   _____   to termin(ate   _LSR_

1. calibrating _____	7. his privacy _____
2. belated _____	8. berating _____
3. with obstinacy _____	9. some inaccuracies _____
4. to locate _____	10. excruciating _____
5. intermediate _____	11. to restate _____
6. we disseminated _____	12. a calculator _____

What is the rule?

Left Stress Rule

For words with left rule endings, stress the left syllable.

---

to gráduate   the pérpetrator   indetérminacy   líteracy

NOTE: See Appendix 2, section D, for patterns predicting the sounds of stressed vowels in the left syllable.

☞ **EXERCISE 3.** Left Stress Rule Words
a. Identify the key and left syllable of each word.
b. Mark the major stress.
c. Read each word or phrase aloud.

Examples: to términate   insínuated

1. to expurgate	4. intimidated	7. the intimacies
2. accommodating	5. determinacy	8. degeneracy
3. with efficacy	6. she collaborated	9. incriminating

10. so obstinate	13. fumigating	16. enumerated
11. his candidacy	14. we illuminated	17. a demonstrator
12. a circulator	15. the confederacy	18. incinerated

CAUTION! There are twelve common *at* + B words stressed on the -*at*. They all have a prefix to the left of the -*at* + B. In order to make sure that you do not use the Left Stress Rule with these words, you should learn them carefully.

unabáted	uninflated	overinflate	overate
undebated	unrelated	overrate	underrate
unsedated	interrelated	overstate	understate

☛ **EXERCISE 4.**   a. Mark the stress on the words above. The first one is done for you.
b. Read each word aloud.

☛ **EXERCISE 5.**   Synthesizing Word Stress Rules

LSR = Left Stress Rule   KSR = Key Stress Rule
VSR = V/VC Stress Rule   PSR = Prefix Stress Rule

For each word,
a. If you haven't studied the rule, put a question mark (?) on the line.
b. If you have studied the rule,
• Identify it: LSR, VSR, KSR, or PSR.
• Underline the key syllable.
• Mark the major stress.
• Read each word or phrase aloud.

Examples:

to invígorate	LSR	to continue	?
períphery	PSR	offíciating	KSR

1. to illuminate	_____	5. repudiated	_____
2. so luminous	_____	6. approximated	_____
3. the lunacy	_____	7. so proximal	_____
4. a luminary	_____	8. in proximity	_____

9. a celebration _____   19. to generate _____

10. celebrated _____   20. generic _____

11. preliminary _____   21. so generational _____

12. the prelacy _____   22. too generous _____

13. advocacy _____   23. his celibacy _____

14. advocating _____   24. deliciously _____

15. advisory _____   25. the delicacies _____

16. a delegacy _____   26. illusory _____

17. a delegation _____   27. so illustrious _____

18. delegated _____   28. an illustrator _____

Exceptions and Variability

EXCEPTIONS

1. These common words are stressed on the key syllable.

	-*ócracy*, e.g.			
to prolóngate	aristócracy	conspíracy	diplómacy	appéllate (Adj.)
to elóngate	demócracy	conspírator	suprémacy	
	also, bureáucracy			

2. Others

to álienate   to decáffeinate   pómegranate (N.)

VARIABILITY

A few words are stressed variably on the key or left.

| Verbs: | to infiltrate | to acclimate | to inculcate |
| Adjectives: | consummate | distillate | condensate |

W-8

PREFIX STRESS
RULE PATTERNS

W-8A. Prefixes and Stress

PATTERNS

This section, Word Stress Domains W-8A, introduces the Prefix Stress Rule. In order to use the rule, you need to identify prefixes in words. You will be able to use prefix information and the Prefix Stress Rule to assign major stress to the correct syllable in many words.

Prefixes are special syllables that can be added to the beginning of a word (or stem) to contribute to the word's meaning. You will look at two types of prefixes: neutral prefixes and regular prefixes.

You are probably already familiar with most of the prefixes you will be learning. Although there are other prefixes in English, the prefixes in sets 1–5 play an important role in the Prefix Stress Rule.

Prefixes

Prefixes are special spellings attached in front of a stem and function to alter the meaning of the stem.

Neutral prefixes are ignored when analyzing words.

Regular prefixes are relevant in the left syllable.

You will also be introduced to the Prefix Stress Rule in this lesson. In Word Stress Domains W-8B and W-8C, you will learn more about the prefix rule endings and where the key syllable is.

In this unit, we are concentrating on identifying the prefixes. So we will underline the key for you when it is relevant.

> **Set 1: Neutral Prefixes**
>
> *counter-/contra-, inter-/intro-,*
> *extra-, over-, retro-, super-*

Neutral prefixes have two distinguishing characteristics.

- Neutral prefixes all have two syllables.
- Neutral prefixes, like neutral endings, are ignored when determining word stress. That is, you should not consider them when analyzing a word.

Prefix	+ Stem	= New Word	Meaning
counter-	active	counteractive	acting against
inter-	active	interactive	acting between or among
over-	active	overactive	too active
retro-	active	retroactive	activated to a prior time
super-	sensory	supersensory	above the senses, spiritual
extra-	sensory	extrasensory	beyond the senses

☛ **EXERCISE 1.**　　a. Is there a neutral prefix in the word?
- If there is, put a line through it: ——————-.
- If not, write the word *none*.

b. Read each word aloud. The stress is marked for you.

Examples:
~~contra~~díctive _____　　incísive _none_

1. overapprehénsive _____
2. supervísory _____
3. condúcive _____
4. recóvery _____
5. contraindícative _____
6. exclúsive _____
7. introdúctory _____

8. extraórdinary _____
9. suppórtive _____
10. counterintúitive _____
11. intercéssory _____
12. óvulatory _____
13. retrospéctive _____
14. incítatory _____

Set 2: Regular Prefixes

de-, re-, pre-, pro-, per-

Prefix	+	Stem	=	New Word	Meaning
re-		tain ("hold")		retain	to hold back or keep for oneself
de-		tain		detain	to hold back or keep away
per-		tain		pertain	to hold through or belong
pre-		war		prewar	before a war
pro-		war		pro-war	in favor of a war

Regular prefixes have these distinguishing characteristics.

1. Regular prefixes have one syllable.
2. Regular prefixes can occur in different positions in the word. We will focus on regular prefixes that occur in the left syllable.
3. If the left syllable contains **all** of a regular prefix, or the **vowel** of a regular prefix, we say that a regular prefix is present there.
   In these examples the prefix *re-* is in the left syllable, even though only the *e-* has a wavy line under it: r<u>e</u>spond, corr<u>e</u>spond, disr<u>e</u>spect.
   In these examples, the prefix *per-* is in the left syllable: p<u>er</u>tain, app<u>er</u>tain.
4. Regular prefixes should be considered **after** neutral prefixes. For example, *re-* is not a regular prefix when it is part of *retro-*, and *per-* is not a regular prefix when it is part of *super-*.

Now you are ready to see how the Prefix Stress Rule works. Remember that the prefix rule endings are described in Word Stress Domains W-8B and W-8C.
   For words with prefix rule endings, the following rule applies.

Prefix Stress Rule

When no part of a prefix is in the left syllable, stress left.
If you can't stress left, stress the key.

~~inter~~áctive	~~extra~~sénsory	refínery	apprehénsive	unprovócative
inquísitive	cátegory	mónastery	appósitive	spéculative

☛ **EXERCISE 2.**   a. Identify the left syllable with a wavy line ($\sim$). The key is marked for you.
b. Put a line through any neutral prefixes: ————.
c. If all or a part of a set 2 prefix is in the left syllable, write out the prefix.
d. If no part of a prefix is in the left syllable, write the word *none*.
e. Mark the stress.
f. Read each word aloud.

Examples:

| unpredíctive | _pre-_ | párcenary | _none_ |

1. prohibitive   _____   7. retrogressive   _____

2. refutatory   _____   8. primitive   _____

3. supervisory   _____   9. perfunctory   _____

4. reproductive   _____   10. overdefensive   _____

5. reiterative   _____   11. depository   _____

6. overapprehensive _____   12. unresponsive   _____

Set 3: Regular Prefixes

ad-, ab-, ob-, sub-

Prefix	+	Stem	=	New Word	Meaning
ob-		ject ("throw")		object	to throw in the way of, oppose
ab-		ject		abject	thrown down, despondent
ad-		join		adjoin	to join toward or next to
sub-		join		subjoin	to join under, to append

☞ **EXERCISE 3.**   a. Identify the left syllable with a wavy line (〰). The key is marked for you.
b. Put a line through any neutral prefixes: ————.
c. If all or a part of a set 3 prefix is in the left syllable, write out the prefix.
d. If no part of a prefix is in the left syllable, write the word *none*.
e. Mark the stress.
f. Read each word aloud.

Examples:

nonabsórptive   _ab-_   árbitrary   _none_

1. advisory   _____   7. nonadhesive   _____

2. inoperative   _____   8. subliterature   _____

3. subcurative   _____   9. apothecary   _____

4. ambulatory   _____   10. overobsessive   _____

5. observatory   _____   11. subversive   _____

6. superabrasive _____   12. sumptuary   _____

Set 4: Regular Prefixes

in-, con-, com-, ex-, dis-

Prefix +	Stem	= New Word	Meaning
in-	clude ("close")	include	to enclose within
con-	clude	conclude	to close together, finish
com-	pel ("drive")	compel	to drive or force together
ex-	pel	expel	to drive out, eject
dis-	pel	dispel	to drive away, scatter

NOTE 1: The forms *con-, ex-,* and *in-* are not regular prefixes when they are part of the neutral prefixes *contra-, extra-, inter-,* and *intro-*.

NOTE 2: The form *in-* is a prefix in the left syllable only when *in-* **begins** a word or when it is preceded by a neutral prefix. *in-* is not a prefix when it is preceded by other letters.

Prefix in Left	**No Prefix in Left**
indicative	v**in**dicative
super**in**tensive	def**in**itive

☞ **EXERCISE 4.**
   a. Identify the left syllable with a wavy line (〰). The key is marked for you.
   b. Put a line through any neutral prefixes: ————.
   c. If all or a part of a set 4 prefix is in the left syllable, write out the prefix.
   d. If no part of a prefix is in the left syllable, write the word *none.*
   e. Mark the stress.
   f. Read each word aloud.

Examples:

exclúsive	*ex-*	córonary	*none*
1. intrusive	_____	7. dispensary	_____
2. intercessory	_____	8. conducive	_____
3. compulsory	_____	9. extraordinary	_____
4. dysentery	_____	10. overinclusive	_____
5. exemplary	_____	11. discovery	_____
6. infinitive	_____	12. contradictory	_____

Set 5: Alternate Forms of Regular Prefixes

The following prefixes are alternative forms of regular prefixes you have already seen. They are easily recognized because of the double consonant letter (*ff, pp,* etc.). Therefore, when you see double consonants in the left syllable, it is an excellent clue to a prefix.

Furthermore, although it does not have a double letter, *im-* before *p* is also a prefix: *improper, impose,* etc. This is an alternate form of *in-*.

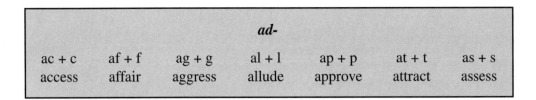

			ad-			
ac + c	af + f	ag + g	al + l	ap + p	at + t	as + s
access	affair	aggress	allude	approve	attract	assess

		ob-		
	oc + c	of + f	op + p	
	occur	offend	oppose	

con-	
col + l	cor + r
collapse	correct

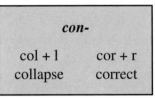

	in-	
il + l		im + p
illumine		impress

ex-
ef + f
effect

dis-
dif + f
diffuse

sub-
suc + c
succeed

NOTE: In these cases, the second consonant is not part of the prefix but is a clue that the first one belongs to a prefix.

☛ **EXERCISE 5.**   a. Identify the left syllable with a wavy line (⌣). The key is marked for you.
b. If all or a part of a set 5 prefix is in the left syllable, write out the prefix.
c. If no part of a prefix is in the left syllable, write the word *none.*
d. Mark the stress.
e. Read each word aloud.

Examples: illúsory   __il-__   ámbulatory   __none__

unsuccéssive   __suc-__

1. attractive   _____   8. eliminatory   _____

2. ordinary   _____   9. offensive   _____

3. effrontery   _____   10. actuary   _____

4. unimpressive   _____   11. corrosive   _____

5. imaginary   _____   12. alliterative   _____

6. applicative   _____   13. accessory   _____

7. diffusive   _____   14. caricature   _____

Summary: Prefixes

Learn to recognize the following prefixes in words.

Neutral: *counter-/contra-, inter-/intro-, extra-, over-, retro-, super-*

Regular: *de-, re-, pre-, pro-, per-, ad-, ab-, ob-, sub-, in-, con-, com-, ex-, dis-*
Remember, *in-* is a prefix only when it begins a word or when it is after a neutral prefix.

Alternate Forms

ac + c	af + f	ag + g	al + l	ap + p	at + t	as + s
oc + c	of + f	op + p	col + l	cor + r		
dif + f	ef + f	il + l	im + p	suc + c		

☞ **EXERCISE 6.**
  a. Identify the left syllable with a wavy line ($\smile$). The key is marked for you.
  b. Put a line through any neutral prefixes: ————.
  c. If all or a part of a regular prefix is in the left syllable, write out the prefix.
  d. If no part of a prefix is in the left syllable, write the word *none.*
  e. Mark the stress.
  f. Read each word aloud.

Examples:

~~over~~defénsive   _de-_   apóthecary   _none_

1. illusory   _____   9. collusive   _____

2. nonadhesive   _____   10. incitory   _____

3. dispensary   _____   11. assumptive   _____

4. successive   _____   12. interjectory   _____

5. statutory   _____   13. affirmative   _____

6. retroactive   _____   14. investigatory   _____

7. submissive   _____   15. oppressive   _____

8. superinductive   _____   16. ambulatory   _____

17. compulsive _____

18. provocative _____

19. itinerary _____

20. abstractive _____

21. obligatory _____

22. personative _____

23. consumptive _____

24. illuminative _____

25. allusive _____

26. propulsive _____

27. countersignature _____

28. expiratory _____

29. occlusive _____

30. overprotective _____

31. extrasensory _____

32. refinery _____

33. indecisive _____

34. supervisory _____

35. aggressive _____

36. corollary _____

W-8B. Prefix Rule Endings
-ary, -ery, -ory, -ive

PATTERNS

In this lesson, you will learn more about the Prefix Stress Rule (PSR) and focus on four prefix rule endings: *-ary, -ery, -ory,* and *-ive.* Before you begin this lesson, be sure you can recognize all of the prefixes presented in Word Stress Domains W-8A.

What words does the Prefix Stress Rule apply to?

- The Prefix Stress Rule applies to nouns and adjectives that end in *-ary, -ery, -ory,* and *-ive.* These are prefix rule endings.

    Examples:

boundary	bribery	theory	pensive
bound(ary	brib(ery	the(ory	pens(ive
pituitary	monastery	category	infinitive
pituit(ary	monast(ery	categ(ory	infinit(ive
infirmary	refinery	advisory	objective
infirm(ary	refin(ery	advis(ory	object(ive

- The Prefix Stress Rule also applies to *-aries, -eries, -ories,* and *-ives* plurals.

bound(aries	brib(eries	the(ories	object(ives

- Note that *-iary* is a key rule ending. Words with this spelling are stressed by the Key Stress Rule, **not** the Prefix Stress Rule. For example, *pecuniary, topiary.* Furthermore, *-ionary* is also a key rule ending and requires the Key Stress Rule.
- The endings *-atory* and *-ative* will be treated in Word Stress Domains W-8C.

☞ **EXERCISE 1.** Identifying Prefix Stress Rule Words
Is the word a Prefix Stress Rule word?
a. If it is,
- Write PSR.
- Mark off the prefix rule ending with an open parenthesis.
b. If it is not, put a line through it: ————.

Examples:

~~intermediary~~ _____   deposit(ory   _PSR_

1. exemplary _____   8. tertiary _____

2. idolatry _____   9. expository _____

3. categories _____   10. forgery _____

4. subsidiary _____   11. economize _____

5. transitive _____   12. weaponries _____

6. peripheries _____   13. misery _____

7. subversive _____   14. discretionary _____

Where is the key syllable?

Use the Key Search Strategy. The key syllable is immediately to the left of the *-ary, -ery, -ory,* and *-ive* prefix rule endings, as underlined.

bound<u>a</u>ry	br<u>i</u>bery	th<u>eo</u>ry	p<u>e</u>nsive
pitu<u>i</u>tary	mon<u>a</u>stery	cat<u>e</u>gory	infin<u>i</u>tive
inf<u>i</u>rmary	ref<u>i</u>nery	adv<u>i</u>sory	obj<u>e</u>ctive

REMINDER: The key consists of all adjacent vowel letters and all following consonant letters up to the prefix rule ending. Remember to include only the V of *i*V and *u*V spellings.

_i_V Spellings	**_u_V Spellings**
*ia, io, iu, ien*C, *iet*	*ua, uo, ue, ui*
di<u>e</u>tary	pitu<u>i</u>tary

Where is the left syllable?

Use the Left Search Strategy. The left syllable is immediately to the left of the key. It includes one vowel letter and any consonants up to the key, as in the examples underlined with a wavy line (⌣⌣).

boundary	bribery	theory	pensive
pituitary	monastery	category	infinitive
infirmary	refinery	advisory	objective

What is the rule?

For words with prefix rule endings, the following rule applies.

Prefix Stress Rule

When no part of a prefix is in the left syllable, stress left.
If you can't stress left, stress the key.

---

boúndary	bríbery	théory	pénsive
pitúitary	mónastery	cátegory	infínitive
infírmary	refínery	advísory	objéctive

NOTE: See Appendix 2, section D, for patterns predicting the sounds of stressed vowels in the left syllable.

☞ **EXERCISE 2.** Prefix Stress Rule Words
a. Separate the prefix rule ending with an open parenthesis.
b. Identify the key and left syllable in each word.
c. Circle the stress command: Key or Left.
d. Mark the major stress.
e. Read each word or phrase aloud.

Examples: exémpl(ary (Key) Left   depósit(ory   Key (Left)

1. an infirmary	Key Left	5. punitory	Key Left
2. his savagery	Key Left	6. inquisitively	Key Left
3. victories	Key Left	7. an artery	Key Left
4. ineffective	Key Left	8. overillusory	Key Left

9. misery	Key	Left	13. compulsory	Key	Left
10. so diminutive	Key	Left	14. unitary	Key	Left
11. effrontery	Key	Left	15. retroactive	Key	Left
12. an emissary	Key	Left	16. secondary	Key	Left

NOTE 1: Words ending in *-mentary* form a special stress class. When only one syllable precedes the *-mentary,* the stress goes on that first syllable. When there is more than one syllable to the left of the *-mentary,* stress goes on the key (containing *-ment*).

Stress Left
(one syllable left of *-ment*)

frágmentary
ségmentary

Stress Key *(ment)*
(more than one syllable left)

compleméntary
eleméntary

NOTE 2: Adjectives ending in *-ary* may become *-arily* adverbs. Stress is variable among *-arily* adverbs. It may fall on *-árily* or on the syllable where it would fall without the *-ly.*

customárily   voluntárily
or   or
cústomarily   vóluntarily

☛ **EXERCISE 3.**   Prefix Stress Rule Words
a. Identify the key and left syllable in each word.
   • For *-ery, -ary, ory,* circle the stress command: Key or Left.
   • For *-arily,* choose one of the correct stress options.
b. Mark the major stress.
c. Read each word or phrase aloud.

Examples: légendary   Key (Left)   adúltery   (Key) Left

1. a tributary	Key	Left	6. chancellery	Key	Left
2. competitive	Key	Left	7. so extraordinarily	Key	Left
3. necessarily	Key	Left	8. supplementary	Key	Left
4. distilleries	Key	Left	9. transitive	Key	Left
5. so complimentary	Key	Left	10. a refractory	Key	Left

11. a commentary	Key	Left		16. so ordinary	Key	Left
12. cemeteries	Key	Left		17. supervisory	Key	Left
13. abusively	Key	Left		18. temporarily	Key	Left
14. a seminary	Key	Left		19. forgery	Key	Left
15. extensively	Key	Left		20. a contraceptive	Key	Left

☞ **EXERCISE 4.**   Synthesizing Word Stress Rules

LSR = Left Stress Rule   KSR = Key Stress Rule
VSR = V/VC Stress Rule   PSR = Prefix Stress Rule

For each word,
a. If you haven't studied the rule, put a question mark (?) on the line.
b. If you have studied the rule,
   • Identify it: LSR, VSR, KSR, or PSR.
   • Underline the key syllable.
   • Mark the major stress.
   • Read each word or phrase aloud.

Examples: ex<u>émpl</u>ary   __PSR__   ex<u>émpl</u>ify   __LSR__

     an example   __?__   exemplific<u>á</u>tion   __KSR__

1. the notaries	_____		11. a luminary	_____
2. with notoriety	_____		12. a secretary	_____
3. notification	_____		13. secretarial	_____
4. momentous	_____		14. infinity	_____
5. momentary	_____		15. an infinitive	_____
6. so definitive	_____		16. the libraries	_____
7. a definition	_____		17. a librarian	_____
8. a dignitary	_____		18. arbitration	_____
9. so dignified	_____		19. arbitrator	_____
10. so luminous	_____		20. arbitrary	_____

Exceptions

-ary	*-ery*		*-ive*	
ádversary	présbytery	ádjective	sedúctive	eléctive
dísciplinary	artíllery	gerúndive	seléctive	elúsive
canáry	machínery	súbstantive	transgréssive	erósive
véterinary		ádditive	transmíssive	evásive
annivérsary	*-ory*	vindíctive	intérpretive	erúptive
vocábulary	állegory			
heréditary	ínventory			
	répertory			
	diréctory			
	-díctory, e.g., benedíctory			
	-fáctory, e.g., satisfáctory			

W-8C. Prefix Rule Endings
-ative, -atory, -ature

PATTERNS

In this lesson, you will learn three more prefix rule endings: *-ative, -atory,* and *-ature.* Before you begin this lesson, be sure you can recognize all of the prefixes in Word Stress Domains W-8A.

What words does the Prefix Stress Rule apply to?

- The Prefix Stress Rule stresses words with these prefix rule endings: *-ative, -atory,* and *-ature.* They all have at least one syllable to the left of the *-at.*

    Examples:

narrative	vibratory	signature
narr(ative	vibr(atory	sign(ature
communicative	circulatory	literature
communic(ative	circul(atory	liter(ature
indicative	observatory	implicature
indic(ative	observ(atory	implic(aturc

- The *-ative* and *-atory* prefix rule endings must be carefully distinguished from the *-ive* and *-ory* endings (Word Stress Domains W-8B). When analyzing such words, it is important to check for the longer endings first. Then the stress can be predicted accurately.
- Remember that words with the key rule endings *-iative, -iatory,* and *-iature* are stressed by the Key Stress Rule, not the Prefix Stress Rule.

☞ EXERCISE 1.   Identifying Prefix Stress Rule Words
   a. If the word is a Prefix Stress Rule word,
      • Write PSR.
      • Mark off the prefix rule ending with an open paren-
        thesis.
      ! Be careful to distinguish -*ative* and -*ive* and -*atory* and
        -*ory.*
   b. If it is not a Prefix Stress Rule word, put a line through
      it: ————.

Examples:

   a ~~calculator~~ _____   a labor(atory   _PSR_

   1. miniature   _____   7. alliterative   _____

   2. legislature _____   8. retaliatory   _____

   3. appreciative _____   9. curvature   _____

   4. generative   _____   10. positive   _____

   5. reformatory _____   11. inflammatory   _____

   6. territory   _____   12. conciliatory   _____

Where is the key syllable?

To find the key syllable, use the Key Search Strategy. The key syllable is immediately to the left of the -*ative, -atory,* or -*ature* prefix rule ending.

> REMINDER: The key consists of all adjacent vowel letters and all follow-
> ing consonant letters up to the prefix rule ending. Remember to include
> only the V of *i*V and *u*V spellings.

*i*V Spellings	*u*V Spellings
*ia, io, iu, ien*C, *iet*	*ua, uo, ue, ui*

Where is the left syllable?

To find the left syllable, use the Left Search Strategy. The left syllable is immediately to the left of the key.

na̲rrative	vi̲bratory	si̲gnature
commu̱nicative	circu̱latory	li̲terature
i̲ndicative	o̲bservatory	i̲mpli̱cature

What is the rule?

For words with prefix rule endings, the following rule applies.

Prefix Stress Rule

When no part of a prefix is in the left syllable, stress left.
If you can't stress left, stress the key.

---

nárrative	víbratory	sígnature
commúnicative	círculatory	líterature
indícative	obsérvatory	implícature

NOTE 1: Words ending in *-mentative* are stressed on the key: *arguménta-tive*.

NOTE 2: See Appendix 2, section D, for patterns predicting the sounds of stressed vowels in the left syllable.

☞ **EXERCISE 2.** Prefix Stress Rule Words
a. Separate off the prefix rule ending with an open paren-thesis.
b. Identify the key and left syllable in each word.
c. Circle the stress command: Key or Left.
d. Mark the major stress.
e. Read each word aloud.

Examples:

consérv(ative	(Key)	Left	líter(ature	Key	(Left)
1. generative	Key	Left	7. indicative	Key	Left
2. procrastinatory	Key	Left	8. exclamatory	Key	Left
3. an oratory	Key	Left	9. hallucinatory	Key	Left
4. derogatory	Key	Left	10. vibratory	Key	Left
5. alimentative	Key	Left	11. provocative	Key	Left
6. musculature	Key	Left	12. caricature	Key	Left

13. inoperative   Key   Left   16. conservatory   Key   Left

14. improvisatory   Key   Left   17. speculative   Key   Left

15. prelature   Key   Left   18. administrative   Key   Left

☞ **EXERCISE 3.**   Synthesizing Word Stress Rules
LSR = Left Stress Rule   KSR = Key Stress Rule
VSR = V/VC Stress Rule   PSR = Prefix Stress Rule

For each word,
a. If you haven't studied the rule, put a question mark (?) on the line.
b. If you have studied the rule,
   • Identify it: LSR, VSR, KSR, or PSR.
   • Underline the key syllable.
   • Mark the major stress.
   • Read each word or phrase aloud.

Examples:
   admínistrative   _PSR_   administrátion   _KSR_

   to administer   _?_   the mínistry   _LSR_

1. the legislature   _____   11. various   _____

2. a legality   _____   12. imagery   _____

3. appellative   _____   13. imaginative   _____

4. an appellation   _____   14. generic   _____

5. the temperature   _____   15. generative   _____

6. *temperate zone   _____   16. generality   _____

7. so temporal   _____   17. argumentation   _____

8. so temporary   _____   18. argumentative   _____

9. variative   _____   19. indicative   _____

10. variability   _____   20. indication   _____

---

*compound noun

Exceptions and Variability

EXCEPTIONS

-ative

accómmodative	evócative	íntegrative	própagative
cónsecrative	exággerative	ínnovative	régulative
colláborative	décorative	nonnátive	réplicative
corróborative	intérpretative	procreátive	supérlative

-atory

ádulatory
corróboratory
dédicatory
délegatory
recómbinatory
súpplicatory

-ature

coféature

VARIABILITY

The following words can be stressed either on the key or the left syllable.

-ative

applicative	contemplative
combinative	denotative
computative	explicative
concentrative	illustrative
connotative	pejorative

-atory

advocatory
indicatory
laboratory
obligatory
preparatory
respiratory

APPENDIXES

The following resources supplement the material in *Speechcraft.*

Appendix 1: Suggestions for Instructors

Special Features of *Speechcraft*

1. Contextualized pronunciation practice. The materials are especially designed to help language learners improve their pronunciation for their own professional or academic contexts.

   - At the discourse level, the content of the practice dialogs and passages is typical of the specified discourse community.
   - At the word level, students apply useful stress patterns to specific vocabulary from their own fields and to the general lexicon of their professional or academic community.
   - The Appendix sections of the workbooks contain useful practice projects in (App. 1) that allow students to apply what they learn to their own contexts in meaningful communication situations.

2. Students' responsibility for improving. While the instructor can provide models, patterns, and some opportunity for practice in class, the majority of pronunciation learning takes place outside of class, when students apply the patterns in their own private practice, called "covert rehearsal." Two activities that directly encourage covert rehearsal are the following.

   a. "Read each word (or phrase or dialog) aloud." This or a similar instruction is incorporated into almost every written assignment in *Speechcraft*. The patterns for prediction are useful only when students apply and internalize them in their own speech. Therefore students must bear the responsibility for reading the exercises aloud on their own.
   b. Tape-recording the written assignments. This activity reinforces the students' responsibility for their own improvement. During tape-recording, students can rehearse, listen to, and correct their own speech. Tapes that are turned in as homework make students even more accountable for their own rehearsal time. They also provide valuable feedback to the instructor regarding students' progress.

Furthermore, the textbook and the workbooks provide answers to their respective Discourse Level and Word Level items in the Appendix section (App. 3) to encourage students to take responsibility for their own learning.

3. Prediction of patterns. In addition to supporting the more traditional pronunciation goals of oral production and aural perception, *Speechcraft* also provides simple rules to predict patterns of pronunciation students should use. One result of this approach is that there is written homework in which the students practice using the patterns. Since this is a somewhat unique practice for an oral skills class, students should be guided carefully in this work. They should also repeatedly be encouraged to read the assignments carefully; they contain critical points that are needed to do the exercises well.

Use of *Speechcraft*

While it is the case that the components of pronunciation are inextricably related, the treatment of them in *Speechcraft* provides maximum flexibility for the instructor. ESL instructors in different teaching contexts have varying amounts of time to spend on pronunciation. Sometimes, an entire course is devoted to pronunciation issues; other times, pronunciation is one part of the course or training curriculum. Furthermore, students have different pronunciation needs. For example, some students need intensive word level work; some need intensive work on discourse level rhythm; some need both. With *Speechcraft,* instructors are free to tailor the types and amounts of pronunciation instruction to their students' own particular needs.

The separation of *Speechcraft* into a core textbook and workbooks enhances *Speechcraft*'s flexibility. The interrelationship between the textbook and the workbooks is depicted in the Preface.

The introductory topics—Groundwork (in the core text) and the Academic or Professional Terms (in the workbooks)—however, must be completed before proceeding with the rest of the text. Groundwork provides an important introduction to the rest of the topics, and later lessons rely on an understanding of this material. Students also must compile their lists of terms right away—they will use these terms in exercises throughout the text.

The two main sections of *Speechcraft,* Discourse Level Topics and Word Level Topics, can be used together in a course or independently. In an optimal teaching environment, students would spend class time each day on discourse and words; thus the relationship between discourse rhythm and word rhythm is reinforced.

Within each section, there is also flexibility, as well as some necessary hierarchy of sections. The Discourse Level Topics can be selected in any order desired, but Discourse Foundations must precede Discourse Domains.

Similarly, in Word Level Topics, the Word Foundations lessons in the textbook (W-1–W-4) must be completed before the word stress rules (excluding W-9, Stress of Constructions in the workbooks). Word Foundations lay out essential principles that are necessary for understanding Word Stress Domains. After Word Foundations, instructors are free to proceed in Word Stress Domains with the word stress rules in any order, according to the needs of their particular students. However, within each word stress unit (W-5, W-6, W-7, W-8), the first section (A) must be completed before proceeding with the subsequent section(s); like Word Foundations, it provides information that is essential for the other section(s) in the unit.

The oral practice projects in the Appendix sections of the workbooks (App. 1) can be integrated into the syllabus as desired. These projects provide an opportunity for student-generated, field-specific, natural language practice.

Fitting Lessons Together

The topics in *Speechcraft* can form the basis of a semester-long course or can be selected and integrated as needed into a more general syllabus.

Organizing a Semester-Long Course: An Example

Following is a sample syllabus for a sixteen-week, three-hour-per-week course, covering word level, discourse level, and sound level topics. The selection of topics provides a general sampling of the topics in *Speechcraft*.

You will see that vowel and consonant work is integrated into the syllabus. In many cases the target sound is related to a word level topic. Because there are ample materials available elsewhere for vowel and consonant practice, they are not included in *Speechcraft*. Instructors are encouraged to consult other resources to find appropriate sound level work to supplement *Speechcraft*'s rhythm work. Instructors would also create the quizzes for their class.

Not all of the lessons are covered in the sample syllabus. Because *Speechcraft*'s coverage is so extensive, most instructors will select just those topics that are of greatest relevance to their own students' needs. It is probably unrealistic to attempt to cover the entire text in one semester.

The italicized topics are prerequisite to later content. Unitalicized topics are suggested topics that may be rearranged or replaced by other topics in *Speechcraft*.

DAY	WORD LEVEL	DISCOURSE LEVEL	SOUND LEVEL	OTHER
1	*Course Introduction* *Preview: G-1. Purpose and Scope*			
2	*Discuss: G-1. Purpose and Scope*		*Preview:* *G-2. Sounds*	
3	*Preview: G-3. Words*		*Practice:* *G-2. Sounds*	
4	*Practice:* *G-3. Words*	*Preview:* *G-4. Discourse*	/ɑ/ and /ɔ/	*Assign Academic or* *Professional Terms*
5		*Practice:* *G-4. Discourse*	/ɑ/ and /ɔ/	
6	*Discuss: W-1.* *Word Stress Rules* *Preview: W-2.* *Neutral, Basic*	*Practice: G-4.* *Discourse*	/ɑ/ and /ɔ/	
7	*Practice: W-2.* *Neutral, Basic* *Preview: W-3.* *Sounds of Endings*	*D-1. Message Units*		Assign Oral Practice Project 1 (App. 1 in workbooks)
8	*Practice: W-3.* *Sounds of Endings*	*D-1. Message Units*		Review for QUIZ on endings and sound symbols
9	*Preview W-4. Key,* *Left Syllables* *Practice: W-3.* *Sounds of Endings*	D-2. Rhythm— Alternations		QUIZ
10	*Practice W-4. Key,* *Left Syllables*	D-2. Rhythm— Alternations		
11	Practice: Oral Practice Project 1	D-2. Rhythm— Alternations	/ʃ/	
12	In-Class Presentations: Oral Practice Project 1		/ʃ/	
13	Preview: W-5A. KSR	*D-5. Primary Stress:* *Content Words*	/ʧ/	

DAY	WORD LEVEL	DISCOURSE LEVEL	SOUND LEVEL	OTHER
14	Practice: W-5A. KSR	*D-5. Primary Stress: Content Words*	/tʃ/	Review for QUIZ on endings, *u* and *y*, primary stress
15	Practice: W-5A. KSR	*D-5. Primary Stress: Content Words*	/tʃ/	QUIZ
16	Preview: W-5B. KSR	*D-7. Intonation*	/dʒ/	
17	In-Class Presentations: Oral Practice Project 1			
18	Practice: W-5B. KSR	*D-7. Intonation*	/dʒ/	Assign Oral Practice Project 2 (App. 1 in workbooks)
19		*D-7. Intonation* D-3. Rhythm— Linking	/ʒ/	Review for QUIZ on KSR, primary stress
20		D-3. Rhythm— Linking	/l/	QUIZ
21	Preview: W-6A. VSR W-9A. Compound Nouns 1 (workbooks)	D 4. Rhythm— Trimming	/l/	
22	Preview: W-6A. VSR W-9A. Compound Nouns 1		/r/	
23	In-Class Presentations: Oral Practice Project 2			
24	Practice: W-6A. VSR	*D-6. Primary Stress— Function Words*	/r/	
25		*D-6. Primary Stress— Function Words*	/r/	Review for QUIZ on VSR, primary stress
26		D-13. Info. Q & A (workbooks)		QUIZ
27	In-Class Presentations: Oral Practice Project 2			

DAY	WORD LEVEL	DISCOURSE LEVEL	SOUND LEVEL	OTHER
28	Preview: W-7A. LSR	D-13. Info. Q & A	/v/	
29	Practice: W-7A. LSR	D-11. *Yes/No* Q & A	/v/	
30	Preview: W-7B. LSR	D-11. *Yes/No* Q & A Practice: Oral Practice Project 2	/ey/	
31	Practice: W-7B. LSR	D-10. Choice Q & A	/ey/	
32	Preview: W-8A. PSR	D-10. Choice Q & A	/ey/	Assign Oral Practice Project 3 (App. 1 in workbooks)
33	Practice: W-8A. PSR Preview: W-8B. PSR	D-8. Comparing and Contrasting		
34	Practice: W-8B. PSR	D-8. Comparing and Contrasting		
35	W-9B. Compound Nouns 2 (workbook)		/ʌ/	Review for QUIZ on LSR, PSR, questions
36	W-9B. Compound Nouns 2		/ʌ/	QUIZ
37	Practice: Oral Practice Project 3			
38	In-Class Presentations: Oral Practice Project 3			
39	Review Word Stress Rules		/θ/	
40	W-9D. Compound Numbers		/θ/	
41	Practice Academic or Professional Terms		Vowel Review	
42	Catch-up day			
43	In-Class Presentations: Oral Practice Project 3 Course Conclusion			
44	NO CLASS: Student conferences			

Integrating Topics into a Broader Syllabus: Alternatives

Speechcraft is also adaptable for those courses that only devote a portion of their time to pronunciation—as few as six to ten hours per term. For example, a selection of the pronunciation topics covered could be integrated into a syllabus for a more general ESL course.

The Groundwork sections alone may be sufficient for some classes. After Groundwork, nearly every topic in *Speechcraft* could be extracted and presented without going through the rest of the text. Again, the choice of topics is based on students' needs. There is virtually no end to the possible combinations, but a few are given below as examples of six, twenty, and thirty hours per term.

Six Hours: The Basics
Groundwork G-1–G-4

Ten Hours: Example 1	Ten Hours: Example 2
Groundwork G-1–G-4	Groundwork G-1–G-4
Discourse Level Topics	*Discourse Level Topics*
D-1. Message Units	D-1. Message Units
	D-5. Primary Stress . . . Content Words
Word Level Topics	*Word Level Topics*
Academic or Professional Terms	W-9A. Compound Nouns 1

Twenty Hours: Example 1	Twenty Hours: Example 2
Groundwork G-1–G-4	Groundwork G-1–G-4
Discourse Level Topics	*Discourse Level Topics*
D-1. Message Units	D-2. Rhythm—Alternations
D-3. Rhythm— Linking	D-5. Primary Stress . . . Content Words
D-5. Primary Stress . . . Content Words	D-6. Primary Stress . . . Function Words
D-6. Primary Stress . . . Function Words	D-7. Intonation
D-7. Intonation	D-8. Comparing and Contrasting
	D-10. Choice Questions and Answers
Word Level Topics	*Word Level Topics*
W-1.–W-4. Word Foundations	W-9A. Compound Nouns 1
W-5A. and W-5B. Key Stress Rule: Practice and Review	W-9D. Compound Numbers
W-6A. V/VC Rule Endings *-al, -ous, ic*	

THIRTY HOURS: EXAMPLE 1	THIRTY HOURS: EXAMPLE 2
Groundwork G-1–G-4	Groundwork G-1–G-4
Discourse Level Topics	*Discourse Level Topics*
All	D-2. Rhythm—Alternations
	D-5. Primary Stress . . . Content Words
	D-6. Primary Stress . . . Function Words
	D-7. Intonation
	D-11. *Yes/No* Questions and Answers
	D-13. Information Questions and Answers
Word Level Topics	*Word Level Topics*
Academic or Professional Terms	W-1–W-4. Word Foundations
	W-7A, B. Left Stress Rule: Practice and Review
	W-8A, B, C. Prefix Stress Rule: Practice and Review

The time allotments in the suggestions are approximate and probably represent the minimum amount of time needed. They also assume that students will do homework.

Each topic should be spread out over two or more class meetings. Pronunciation topics should be covered gradually to maximize learning.

Groundwork: Suggestions

1. Groundwork G-1 explains the purpose and scope of *Speechcraft*. G-2 provides an overview of consonants and vowels.
2. Groundwork G-3 and G-4 consist of the following.

   • A written description of some basic aspect of pronunciation for students to read at home. Integrated into these descriptions are brief exercises that students complete as they do the reading.
   • Activities for in-class discussion, review, and practice after the homework.

3. Groundwork G-3 and G-4 are concerned with familiarizing students with the concepts, terminology, and conventions of *Speechcraft*. Familiarization takes place through (a) practice associating the terms with the features of pronunciation they represent and (b) ample listening practice in class. Therefore, the exercises in these Groundwork sections are not typical of the

rest of the exercises in Discourse Level Topics or in Word Level Topics. They may seem rather teacher centered, with little student practice beyond listening and repetition. Instructors and students alike should be aware that this is a necessary part of the learning process and that the proportion of teacher talk to student talk will soon shift to the student. Furthermore, students should be told explicitly not to take notes. The content of the presentation is given in the text for reference, so in class, students should focus on listening and understanding.

4. The basic plan for Groundwork lessons is as follows.

 a. Preview the lesson in class. Instructors should present a brief overview of what students will be learning, including a summary of the topics, with some concrete examples for listening practice. Because students will typically be covering the topics on their own as homework, it is also helpful during the preview to point out key terms and to explain how to do any unfamiliar exercises.
 b. Assign the reading to be done as homework. Again, students should be encouraged to do the written exercises incorporated into the readings.
 c. Review the topic and practice in class. This is an opportunity for students to check their understanding of the material and to practice. Instructors can monitor students' understanding and probe for areas of confusion.

Discourse Level Topics

The Discourse Level Topics are mostly designed to be covered during class time. However, it is also possible to assign students to read over the topic before going through it in class. Students can use *Speechcraft*'s audiotapes to help them practice and internalize the patterns. They can also be assigned to make their own tape recordings of the exercises as a way to increase their private practice time. In most cases, each topic moves as follows.

1. Listening practice. Students listen to a pattern or dialog and get accustomed to the target sounds.
2. Analysis of the pattern. Students discover a rule for predicting when the pattern should occur.
3. Controlled practice with the pattern. Students practice applying the pattern to short phrases, dialogs, or passages and then read them aloud. Dialogs and passages can be practiced in pairs or small groups and monitored by the instructor.
4. Practice in a broader context. These assignments are often prepared outside of class. Students have the opportunity to apply patterns to dialogs and talks they create themselves and/or to identify patterns in naturally occurring speech settings.

Again, it is recommended to break up a discourse level lesson over more than one class hour. Learning is enhanced if students can assimilate the pattern over a period of time, being exposed to it more than once.

Word Level Topics
Word Level Topics W-1–W-4 appear only in the core textbook. W-5–W8 appear in both the textbook and the workbooks. W-9 appears only in the workbooks.

Word Level Topic W-1 provides an overview of the word stress rules. W-2 presents the neutral and basic endings. W-3 discusses the *-s, -'s,* and *-ed* endings.

Word Level Topics W-4–W-8 are organized as follows: **Patterns, Practice,** and **Review.** (The Stress of Constructions sections [W-9] are set up more like the Discourse Level Topics.)

In Patterns (in the core textbook), students learn (a) which sets of words are subject to the stress rule in focus, (b) how to find the key syllable (the starting point for determining the major stress of a word), and (c) what the rule is. Students are also provided with exercises that give them practice using the rule to stress words. Patterns exercises can be done as homework, and students can check their own answers in Appendix 3.

The last exercise in each Patterns section in W-5–W7, W-8B, and W-8C has a special function, in that it includes words from other stress rule categories. This helps students learn to distinguish the domains of different word stress rules. It also illustrates the power of the system to explain the stress shifts of words with the same root, e.g., *strátegy* vs. *stratégic, unanímity* vs. *unánimous.* Because other word stress rules may or may not have been covered at this point, students are asked to put a question mark by the words whose stress rule they have not studied.

The Practice component (in the workbooks) provides contextualized practice activities that can be done in class. Students can analyze words and then practice them within the larger discoursal context. Thus the relationship between word rhythm and discourse rhythm is emphasized. The exercises generally progress from controlled to less structured contexts.

During the Practice exercises, students should be monitored carefully for accurate stress on the words stressed by the rule in focus. Misstressed words should be reanalyzed instead of immediately corrected by the instructor (see "Queries" under "Some Special Strategies" below). Instructors can also monitor students' speech for other aspects of word stress, discourse rhythm, and melody that have been covered in class—thus synthesizing the various aspects of speech production required for natural sounding rhythm and melody.

The Review (also in the workbooks) allows students to identify words from their own discourse communities that are stressed by the rule in focus. The Review can be done as homework and tape-recorded. It should be noted that not all students will have a long list of words for each stress rule; this depends to some extent on the lexicon of their individual fields. Instructors can also refer to Appendix 1 in the workbooks for class projects that allow students to practice these terms in speech that they create themselves.

Some Special Strategies

The use of word stress rules will be new to most students. The rules work somewhat like formulas; when they are applied mechanically, they accurately predict the major stress of many thousands of words. (Exceptions are always noted in each lesson.) These two general strategies will provide basic guidelines to use when analyzing words and help students learn to use the rules on their own.

1. Queries. Queries are ordered questions to use every time a student encounters a new word and does not know where the major stress belongs. They can be used in and out of class. Students who learn the queries can use them to analyze the word step by step and to check their own production. Thus the queries also serve as a tool for self-evaluation and self-monitoring.

    The queries are as follows.
    What rule applies?
    Where is the key syllable?
    Where is the left syllable?
    Where is the stress?
    Say the word again!

    For example, if a student misstresses the word *economics* as "ecónomics," the queries might be used as follows.

What rule applies?	V/VC Stress Rule
Where is the key syllable?	econo<u>mic</u>s (underlined)
Where is the left syllable?	econo<u>mic</u>s (wavy line)
Where is the stress?	econó<u>mic</u>s
Say the word again!	"económics"

2. Key and Left Search Strategies. The concepts of the key and left syllable will also be new to students. Although finding the key and left syllables is not difficult, students need guidelines and practice in order to learn to do it naturally. The Key Search Strategy and the Left Search Strategy provide guidance in this part of the analysis. They are explained in Word Foundations W-4. As with the queries, repeated use of these ordered guidelines will enhance students' ability to use the word stress rules with confidence and accuracy.

Appendix 2: Vowel and Consonant Prediction Patterns

Nearly all the vowel and consonant sounds in English words are predictable by looking at how the vowels and consonants are spelled. The relevant clues are combinations of letters, word stress, and information about the position of letters in a word.

Prediction patterns for vowel and consonant sounds can be stated as equations in which spelling information is on the left of an equals sign (=) and the predicted sound is on the right. If you can match the spelling part of the equation to the spelling in a word, you can be quite certain that the sound in the word will be the sound predicted by the pattern. While the vowel and consonant prediction patterns are highly reliable, a few common exceptions should be noted.

To simplify the prediction patterns, certain abbreviations are used.

V	means one vowel letter
C	means one consonant letter
+B	means "before a basic ending"
+K	means "before a key rule ending"
←	means "in the left syllable"
Ø	means silence
/	separates two letters, either of which may be in the spelling pattern
~	separates two different but acceptable pronunciations
<u>Underlining</u>	identifies the part of the pattern for which a prediction is being made.

A full presentation of prediction patterns for vowel and consonant sounds can be found in *Stress in the Speech Stream: The Rhythm of Spoken English, Student Manual* by Wayne B. Dickerson (1989).

A. *U* as a Consonant Letter

When the letter *u* represents a consonant, what does the consonant sound like? These patterns tell you. Use them in the order presented.

Words with *qu*		**Words with *gu***	
1. *qu* + B = Ø	critique, critiqued	1. *gu* + B = Ø	fatigue, fatiguing
2. *qu*V = /w/	quote, requested	2. *ngu*V = /w/	linguist, distinguished
		3. *gu*V = Ø	guess, guitar

Exceptions: *u* is Ø in *bouquet, conquer, liquor, queue, mosquito, etiquette*; *u* is a vowel letter in *ague, ambiguity, ambiguous, argue, contiguity, contiguous.*

B. Stressed Vowels in Key Stress Rule Words

A single vowel letter (V) followed by a single consonant letter (C) in the key syllable is predictable as an unglided (lax) or a glided (tense) vowel using the patterns below. If the vowel is spelled with *i*, it represents the lax vowel, /ɪ/. But if the vowel is spelled with *a, e, o,* or *u,* it is pronounced with the tense vowel sounding like the name of the letter.

1. *í*C + K = /ɪ/			inítial, vícious, affíliated
2. V́C + K = tense	*á*C + K = /ey/		státion, grácious, áviator
	*é*C + K = /iy/		déviate, régional, comédian
	*ó*C + K = /ow/		ópium, explósion, pólio
	*ú*C + K = /uw/		exclúsion, allúvial, dúbious

Exceptions: V́C + K is lax in *battálion, compánion, gládiator, Itálian, nátional, rátional, retáliate, Spániard, váliant, discrétion, espécially, spécial, précious, búnion.* Others are *carburétion* /ey/, *ónion* /ʌ/.

C. Consonant Sounds before Key Rule Endings

The letters *c, g, t, s,* and *x* before a key rule ending regularly represent palatal sounds as follows. Notice that rule 3, which is more specific than rule 4, must be tried before rule 4. Rule 7 shows that there is regional variation in educated speech; either variant is acceptable. Rule 8 applies only if the key rule ending begins with *io.*

1. *c* + K = /ʃ/	artificial, magician, Confucius
2. *g* + K = /dʒ/	religion, collegiate, allegiance
3. *st* + K = /tʃ/	question, Sebastian, celestial
4. *t* + K = /ʃ/	eviction, substantial, martial

5. V*s* + K = /ʒ/   adhesion, Asia, erosion
6. C*s* + K = /ʃ/   convulsion, discussion, Russian
7. *r̠s̠* + K = /ʒ ~ ʃ/   version, excursion, reversion
8. *x* + *io* = /kʃ/   anxious, flexion, noxious

The *i* of the key rule ending is pronounced as either Ø, /y/, or /i/. These pronunciations are predictable by what precedes and follows the *i*V. The patterns are the following. In pattern 10, any combination of a preceding *l* or *n* with a following *n* or *r* is acceptable.

9. *c, g, t, s, x* + *i̠*V = Ø   See the examples in rules 1–8 in section C.
10. *l/n i̠*V *n/r* = /y/   *l i*V *n*: million; *l i*V *r*: familiar; *n i*V *n*: opinion; *n i*V *r*: senior
11. *i̠*V elsewhere predicts /i/   envious, serial, accordion, Scorpio, immediate

D. Stressed Vowels in Left Syllables

The letter *u,* when stressed and followed by a single consonant letter (C), predicts a tense vowel, namely, /uw/. All other single vowel letters (V), when stressed and followed by one consonant letter (C), will be pronounced as a lax (unglided) vowel. The symbol indicating the left syllable position is a leftward pointing arrow (←). Note that when you stress the left syllable you always leave the key syllable with an unstressed, reduced vowel.

1. *ú*C ← = /uw/   commúnicate, lúminary, únify
2. V́C ← = lax   *á*C ← = /æ/   rádical, neutrálity, strátegy
                    *é*C ← = /ɛ/   compétitive, président, féderated
                    *í*C ← = /ɪ/   metículous, partícipant, mínistry
                    *ó*C ← = /ɑ ~ ɔ/   hónorary, óminous, morphólogy

Exceptions: V́C ← is tense in *stratégic, aphásic, básic, orthopédic, anémic, procédural, líbelous.*

E. The Invisible /y/

Certain vowel spellings invite the /y/ consonant to join the vowel. We call these particular spellings **y-ful spellings** and abbreviate them YS. The YS spellings are *eu, ew* (e.g., *feud* / . . . yuw . . . /, *few* / . . . yuw/), and the vowel letter *u* when followed by no consonant letter (e.g., *menu* / . . . yuw/, *annual* /. . . yuw/) or by only one consonant letter and a vowel letter or nonneutral ending (e.g., *unity* /yuw . . . /, *cute* / . . . yuw . . . /). (The VC spelling as in *bus, fun* and the VCC spelling as in *bust, fund* are not YS spellings.) The general rule below uses an underline to indicate that the invisible /y/ goes before the YS spelling.

    1. __YS = /y/   feudal, hewing, unity, music, evaluate, annuity

Sometimes the /y/ is omitted (Ø) before a YS. This occurs when the letter immediately before the YS is either *j, r,* or C*l*: *June, ruin, glue.* The rule is the following.

    2. *j/r/*C*l*__YS = Ø   jewel, Jupiter, true, accrual, pluvial, agglutinate

If the YS is stressed and the consonant letter before the YS is either *t, d, s, x, l,* or *n,* then the invisible /y/ may be acceptably present or absent according to the region in which English is spoken.

    3. *t/d/s/x/l/n* + ÝS = /y ~ Ø/   túne, déw, assúme, resúme, exúde, lúminous, néws

Finally, if the YS is unstressed and the consonant letter before it is either *t, d, s,* or *x,* then the invisible /y/ may be present or may form a palatal consonant: *grádŭate* /. . . dy . . . / or /. . . ʤ . . . /. Five rules state the variation in this case.

    4. *t* + Y̆S = /ty ~ ʧ/   nátŭral, constítŭent, témpĕrătŭre
    5. *d* + Y̆S = /dy ~ ʤ/   indivídŭal, ádŭlatory, árdŭous
    6. V*s* + Y̆S = /zy ~ ʒ/   tréasŭry, cásŭal, vísŭal
    7. C*s* + Y̆S = /sy ~ ʃ/   íssŭable, sénsŭous, tíssŭe
    8. *x* + Y̆S = /ksy ~ kʃ/   lúxŭry, séxŭal, fléxŭous

Exceptions: These words have no invisible /y/: *study, punish, build, built, bury, busy, buy, insulate.*

Appendix 3: Answers to Items

Groundwork

G-2. Sounds: Overview of Vowels and Consonants

1.	wrong	6.	call
2.	jello	7.	pert
3.	match	8.	look
4.	lesioned	9.	load
5.	police	10.	rival

G-3. Beyond Sounds: Overview of the Word Level

Patterns

Exercise 2

1.	2	6.	3
2.	3	7.	3
3.	5	8.	2
4.	1	9.	3
5.	5	10.	4

Practice

Exercise 1

1.	2	6.	4
2.	1	7.	2
3.	2	8.	3
4.	4	9.	4
5.	3	10.	2

Exercise 2

1. vowel length, vowel quality, pitch
2. major stress ′ superfícial
   minor stress ‵ sùperficial
   unstressed ˘ supĕrficiăl

Exercise 3

U: experimental, apparent, dissertation, connect, parallel, biography, symmetrical, nonviolent

S: solution, academic, magnitude, assignment, correlation, confrontational, confidence, parameters

′: experiméntal, appárent, dissertátion, connéct, párallel, biógraphy, symmétrical, nonvíolent, solútion, académic, mágnitude, assígnment, correlátion, confrontátional, cónfidence, parámeters

Exercise 4
   1. the first word

G-4. Beyond Words: Overview of the Discourse Level
Patterns
  Exercise 4
    •   O   O • •   O • O   • O
    B: You'll never believe it. It's "How to manage your time."
  Exercise 5
    'm, 'm, 'm
  Exercise 8
    ↑; ↳, ↓; ↓; ↳, ↳, ↓; ↑; ↓, ↓
Practice
    O: What, like; What (area); Why, taking; What, like do
    •: do, you, to be; (of), are, you, in; are, you, this; do, you, to, for
    ●: called; profession (specialization); class; fun

DISCOURSE LEVEL TOPICS

D-2. Rhythm—Alternations
  Exercise 1
    O: prosperous, fortunes, modest, wise, greatest, fall, lowest, rise
    •: In, be, and, The, may, and, the, may
  Exercise 3
    O: Hope, gain, lessens, pain; quiet, Conscience, sleeps, Thunder, Rest, Guilt, live,
       far, asunder; slip, foot, soon, recover, slip, Tongue, never, get over
    •: of; A, in, but, and; A, of, the, you, may, But, a, of, the, you, may
  Exercise 5
    O: topic, today; What, need, cover, next; Today, going, talk; Let, repeat; say, again,
       sure, remember; Let, say, that, another, way; other, words; put, another, way;
       want, make, clear; This, important, point; sure, get, point, important; example;
       Let, give, example; instance; way; little, topic; Anyway, saying; Now, back,
       what, talking; conclusion; let's, see, summarize; What, conclude, today

D-4. Rhythm—Trimming
  Exercise 2
  In each word, the vowel letter following the stressed vowel (′) should be crossed out,
  e.g., anómalous, cábinet, áverage.
  Exercise 3
  anomaly, dominant, reference, considerable, liberal, summary, difference, literal,
  traditional, different, marginal

Exercise 5

1. intérest
2. privílege
3. listéning
4. evéning
5. What's, avérage, saláry

6. What's, cultúral, différence, and ('n')
7. What's, perfecl
8. excéllent, friendship
9. Who's, promínent, history, him/her
10. What's, first, memóry

Exercise 6

Besl, Sky's, Privíleged, Avérage, 'n'

D-5. Primary Stress—New Information in Content Words

Exercise 1

•: pH, compounds, seven, acid, larger, base, exactly, neutral, example, water

Exercise 3

Sit. 1: (It's) a right (triangle).   •: right
Sit. 2: Physics (was my major).   •: Physics
        Nuclear (physics).   •: Nuclear
Sit. 3: (I have a) few (ideas).   •: few
        But nothing very interesting.   •: interesting

Exercise 4

Sit. 1: What color should (our) chemical solution be?
        Blue | —dark (blue).
        •: solution, blue, dark
Sit. 2: Did (you) read Professor Bond's paper?
        (I) tried, | but (it) was too complicated.
        (Her papers) are always (complicated). (Did you read her) first (paper)? (It
        was) nearly impossible!
        (I) know. (It) took (me) forever.
        •: paper; tried, complicated; always, first, impossible; know, forever
Sit. 3: (I)'m going to interview Clark and Perkins. Do (you) know (them)?
        Yes. (I) met (them) at a conference in July.
        What do (you) think of (them)?
        (I think Clark)'s more experienced than (Perkins). But (they're) both good |
        —really (good).
        •: Perkins, know; Yes, July; think; experienced, good, really
Sit. 4: How would (you) compare Beethoven and Brahms?
        (Brahms) is more romantic than (Beethoven).
        •: Brahms; romantic
Sit. 5: (I)'m looking for a textbook on physiology. (I) found some new (textbooks), |
        but do (you) have any used (ones)?
        (I) don't think (so). (We)'ve already sold (the used ones).
        •: physiology, new, used; think, sold

Sit. 6: (My) <u>company is sending</u> (me) <u>to Albania to do some research</u>.
(That) <u>sounds fascinating</u>. <u>What part of</u> (Albania)?
<u>Tirana</u>. (It)'<u>s the capital</u>. <u>But if</u> (I) <u>had a map</u>, | (I)'<u>m not even sure</u> (I) <u>could</u>
<u>find</u> (Albania).
(It)'<u>s on the Adriatic</u>, | <u>kind of between Yugoslavia and Greece</u>.
(Is)<u>n't</u> (it) <u>communist</u>?
(It) <u>used</u> (to be communist). <u>Now</u> (it's) <u>a democracy</u> | —<u>or at least trying to</u>
<u>become</u> (a democracy).
  ●: research; fascinating, part; Tirana, capital, map, find; Adriatic, Greece;
     communist; used, democracy, become

Sit. 7: (I)'<u>m looking for a speaker for</u> (our) <u>next seminar</u>. <u>Do</u> (you) <u>have any ideas</u>?
<u>What kind of</u> (speaker)?
(I)'<u>d like to find</u> (someone) <u>to talk about computer ethics</u>.
<u>What aspect of</u> (computer ethics)?
<u>Privacy on the Internet</u>.
<u>How about Jane Foster</u>?
(She) <u>might be OK</u>, | <u>but</u> (I) <u>really want</u> (someone) <u>dynamic</u>.
<u>Nancy Park's</u> (dynamic). <u>But</u> (I) <u>wonder if</u> (she)'<u>s available</u>.
(She's) <u>never</u> (available). (Her) <u>schedule's always too full</u>.
  ●: seminar, ideas; kind; ethics; aspect; Internet; Foster; OK, dynamic;
     Parks, available; never, full

Pas. 1: <u>For next week's project</u>, | (you)'<u>ll need the computer</u>. <u>If</u> (you)'<u>ve never used</u>
(the computer), | (you)'<u>ll have to attend a special seminar</u>.
  ●: project, computer, used, seminar

Pas. 2: <u>A morpheme is the basic unit of meaning in a language</u>. <u>There are two major</u>
<u>types of</u> (morphemes). <u>First, let'</u>(s) <u>look at free</u> (morphemes). <u>"Group" is a</u>
(free morpheme). <u>"Child"</u> (is) <u>also</u> (a free morpheme). <u>So</u> (free morphemes
are) <u>independent words</u>.
  ●: language, types, free, "Group", also, words

Pas. 3: <u>The Italian Renaissance began in the late thirteenth century</u>, | <u>and</u> (it) <u>did not</u>
<u>end until the fifteenth</u> (century). <u>Florence was the center of</u> (the Renais-
sance).
  ●: century, fifteenth, center

Exercise 5
  ●: major; chemistry; Really, in- (of inorganic)

Exercise 6
Sit. 1: (I) <u>heard that Max is writing a new book</u>. <u>What's the topic</u>?
<u>Microbiology</u>.
<u>Is</u> (this his) <u>first</u> (book)?
<u>Actually</u>, | (he) <u>also</u> (wrote one) <u>on psycho</u>(biology.)
  ●: book, topic; Microbiology; first; Actually, psycho (of psychobiology)

Sit. 2:   <u>Look</u>. (I) <u>think</u> (we) <u>have a bimodal distribution</u>. <u>There are seven scores of 40 and seven scores of 54</u>.
<u>Actually</u>, | (it)<u>'s uni</u>(modal). (The score of) <u>58 appears nine times</u>.
●: Look, distribution, 4 (of 54); Actually, uni- (of unimodal), times

Sit. 3:   <u>So next let'</u>(s) <u>calculate *d* squared</u>.
<u>No</u>, | <u>first</u> (we) <u>need *r*</u> (squared).
●: squared; No, *r*

Exercise 7
●: opinion, advantageous; higher; higher, right

Exercise 8
Sit. 1 ●: Pennsylvania; Wright; Wright, right
Sit. 2 ●: reasoning, remember; preconventional; preconventional, Thank, second
Sit. 3 ●: dilemma; sheep; sheep, Good, consideration

D-6. Primary Stress—New Information in Function Words

Exercise 1
●: hear, product; June, our; before

Exercise 2
Sit. 1:   (I) <u>hope</u> (you)<u>'ll give me a call</u>. (I) <u>need to talk to</u> (you) <u>about</u> (my) <u>data</u>.
(I will) <u>if</u> (I) <u>can</u>. But (I)<u>'m really busy</u>.
●: call, data; can, busy

Sit. 2:   (I) <u>just finished reading a terrific article</u>.
<u>What was</u> (it) <u>on</u>?
<u>Educational policy in the nineteenth century</u>.
●: article; on; century

Sit. 3:   <u>Do</u> (you) <u>still want to get together tomorrow at 9:00</u>?
<u>Sure</u>. <u>How about at Espresso Royale</u>? (That)<u>'s where</u> (I)<u>'ll be</u>.
●: 9:00; Sure, Royale, be

Sit. 4:   (I) <u>need to get to</u> (your) <u>office</u>. <u>Isn't</u> (it) <u>in Lincoln Hall</u>?
<u>No</u>. But (it's) <u>near</u> (Lincoln Hall). (It's in) <u>the *Science Building</u>.
●: office, Hall; No, near, Science

Sit. 5:   <u>So, when</u> (we) <u>want to find the stress of a word</u>, | (we) <u>should find the key</u>, | <u>then determine the rule</u>?
<u>No</u>. (You find the key syllable) <u>after</u> (you determine the rule).
●: word, key, rule; No, after

Sit. 6:   (We) <u>need someone who can speak either Spanish or French</u>.
(I can speak Spanish) <u>and</u> (French)!
●: French; and

Exercise 3
●: are; fine, you

---

*compound noun

Exercise 5

Sit. 1: <u>The committee just made</u> (their) <u>promotion decisions.</u>
<u>How do</u> (you) <u>know?</u> <u>Are</u> (you) <u>on</u> (it)?
<u>No,</u> | <u>but</u> (I) <u>heard about</u> (it) | <u>from someone who is.</u>
●: promotion; know, on; No, heard, is

Sit. 2: (I) <u>missed the last *staff meeting.</u>
(You) <u>should have been</u> (there). <u>There was a big argument.</u>
●: staff; been, argument

Sit. 3: (I) <u>couldn't find any recent articles on the economy of Ghana.</u>
<u>But there are</u> (some). <u>Look in the *Commerce Library.</u>
●: Ghana; are, Commerce

Sit. 4: <u>There's a fax for</u> (you). (It's) <u>on the desk.</u>
(It) <u>must be</u> (for) <u>you.</u> (It) <u>has</u> (your) <u>name on</u> (it).
●: fax, desk; you, name

Sit. 5: (I) <u>just tried to send a message on e-mail,</u> | <u>but</u> (I) <u>couldn't.</u> (I) <u>can't even access</u> (my) <u>account.</u>
(You) <u>can</u> (send it on) <u>my</u> (account) | <u>if</u> (you) <u>want.</u>
●: e-mail, couldn't, account; my, want

Exercise 6

1. before
2. after
3. before
4. before
5. after
6. before

D-7. Intonation

Exercise 1

↓; ↓; ↓; ↳, ↓; ↑; ↓; ↓, ↳, ↓; ↓

Exercise 5

Sit. 1: L (statement), H (statement question); L (statement); H (statement question); M (nonfinal phrase), L (statement)

Sit. 2: L (command); H (statement question); H (statement question); L (statement), M (list), M (list), L (final element in a list)

WORD LEVEL TOPICS

W-2. Neutral and Basic Endings

Patterns

Exercise 2

1. appreciat(es̸
2. measur(ing instruments̸
3. several occasions̸
4. bring the fe(e
5. decid(edl̸y
6. costl̸y decisions̸
7. critical̸ly injur(ed
8. his colleagu(es̸
9. was includ(ing
10. homogeneous group

---

*compound noun

11. the judg(e's ~~s~~ decision
12. to rally
13. He will succeed.
14. studi(ed biophysic~~s~~
15. to heed the advic(e
16. respectiv(e~~l~~y
17. simultaneous
18. exceed(ing~~l~~y
19. the antonym~~s~~
20. to discuss
21. It annoy(ed us.
22. imping(ed on it
23. stress rul(e~~s~~
24. It'~~s~~ ring(ing.

Practice
  Exercise
    Sit. 1: Truste(e~~s~~, reach(ed; detail~~s~~; wonder(ing
    Sit. 2: Who'~~s~~, favorit(e; It'~~s~~, definit(e~~l~~y, wrot(e
    Sit. 3: hav(e, experienc(e, teach(ing; I'v(e, thre(e, class(e~~s~~, Element~~s~~, Conduct(ing, Beginn(ing, Instrument~~s~~
    Sit. 4: Rica'~~s~~, work(ing, way~~s~~, sav(e, forest~~s~~, hav(e, recent~~l~~y, develop(ed, softwar(e
    Sit. 5: Fox(e~~s~~, ar(e, mammal~~s~~, ar(e, near~~l~~y, tail~~s~~, ar(e, on(e, interest(ing, featur(e~~s~~, Fox(e~~s~~, us(e, tail~~s~~, thes(e, animal~~s~~, balanc(e, messag(e~~s~~

Review
  Exercise
    1. rat(ing system~~s~~
    2. varietal win(e~~s~~
    3. virtual~~l~~y ignor(ed
    4. was injur(ing
    5. Marg(e'~~s~~ opinion
    6. He will need this.
    7. furious
    8. finger~~s~~ and to(e~~s~~
    9. coagulat(e~~s~~
    10. bring som(e paper~~s~~
    11. her critiqu(e~~s~~
    12. a ludicrous request
    13. to dally
    14. conclusiv(e~~l~~y
    15. to digress mark(ed~~l~~y
    16. scor(ed mor(e point~~s~~

W-3. The Sounds of the -s/-'s *and* -ed *Endings*
Patterns
  Exercise 1
    1. /s-z/
    2. /s-z/
    3. ge, /əz/
    4. /s-z/
    5. ch, /əz/
    6. /s-z/
    7. s, /əz/
    8. /s-z/
    9. /s-z/
    10. z, /əz/
    11. /s-z/
    12. sh, /əz/
    13. xe, /əz/
    14. sh, /əz/
    15. /s-z/
    16. /s-z/
    17. s, /əz/
    18. /s-z/
    19. /s-z/
    20. ge, /əz/
    21. che, /əz/
    22. ze, /əz/
    23. /s-z/
    24. /s-z/
    25. ce, /əz/
    26. x, /əz/

Exercise 2

1. d, /əd/	11. /t-d/
2. /t-d/	12. t, /əd/
3. /t-d/	13. /t-d/
4. d, /əd/	14. t, /əd/
5. t, /əd/	15. d, /əd/
6. /t-d/	16. /t-d/
7. d, /əd/	17. /t-d/
8. t, /əd/	18. t, /əd/
9. /t-d/	19. /t-d/
10. d, /əd/	20. /t-d/

Practice

Exercise 1

/s-z/: learns, universities, doctors, cures, lowers, falls, words, notes, chapters, lines, repeats, parts

/əz/: teaches, colleges, nurses, diseases, raises, rises, phrases, messages, verses, pages, memorizes, pieces

Exercise 2

/t-d/: studied, arrived, learned, watched

/əd/: attended, painted, invented, wanted, started

Exercise 3

/s-z/: desks, chairs, students, texts, students', names, policies, grades, students, goals

/əz/: faces, pages, classes

/t-d/: arrived, arranged, introduced, required, called, matched, explained, described, assigned, asked

/əd/: visited, located, listed

W-4. Key Syllables and Left Syllables

Patterns

Exercise 1

1. sch<u>oo</u>l's	9. pr<u>ou</u>dly
2. th<u>ir</u>d	10. adm<u>ir</u>(es
3. s<u>ou</u>nd	11. t<u>im</u>(ing
4. aud<u>it</u>	12. enh<u>anc</u>(e
5. conc<u>ern</u>s	13. end<u>ors</u>(ed
6. app<u>ear</u>(ed	14. st<u>irr</u>(ingly
7. prom<u>ot</u>(ed	15. und<u>aunt</u>(ed
8. gr<u>ow</u>(ing	16. pl<u>eas</u>(e

Exercise 2

1. rep<u>ut</u>(ed*l*y
2. tru<u>ant</u>s
3. rel<u>ax</u>(ing
4. vi<u>and</u>
5. c<u>aus</u>(ing
6. di<u>od</u>(es
7. n<u>eedl</u>(es
8. c<u>oax</u>(ed

9. m<u>ous</u>(e
10. mount<u>ain</u>
11. fort<u>un</u>(e
12. sust<u>ain</u>(ing
13. l<u>augh</u>
14. r<u>uin</u>(ed
15. ach<u>iev</u>(es
16. pliant*l*y

Exercise 3

1. qu<u>ench</u>
2. r<u>ough</u>
3. del<u>ay</u>(ing
4. g<u>ush</u>(ing
5. acqu<u>aint</u>
6. y<u>ell</u>(ing
7. crit<u>iqu</u>(e
8. qu<u>iet</u>(*l*y

9. disob<u>ey</u>(ed
10. year*l*y
11. angu<u>ish</u>
12. g<u>uest</u>'s
13. cr<u>ypt</u>
14. val<u>u</u>(e
15. august*l*y
16. pr<u>ey</u>(ing

Exercise 4

1. e<u>scap</u>(ing
2. int<u>erest</u>(ed
3. str<u>ess</u>
4. h<u>eight</u>
5. req<u>uir</u>(es
6. my<u>thic</u>
7. beg<u>uil</u>(ed
8. pro<u>mot</u>(ed
9. det<u>ermin</u>(e
10. great*l*y

11. ac<u>quir</u>(ed
12. intro<u>duc</u>(ed
13. g<u>uzzl</u>(ed
14. g<u>uess</u>(ed
15. cr<u>uel</u>*l*y
16. sy<u>llabl</u>(c
17. yawns
18. wo<u>nder</u>(ed
19. d<u>uet</u>s
20. t<u>utor</u>(ing

Practice and Review

1. cr<u>am</u>, t<u>est</u>, int<u>erview</u>, m<u>eans</u>, prep<u>are</u>, int<u>ensely</u>, qu<u>ickly</u>, br<u>ief</u>, t<u>ime</u>, <u>event</u>
2. bl<u>ow</u>, cl<u>ass</u>, m<u>eeting</u>, m<u>eans</u>, m<u>iss</u>, pur<u>pose</u>
3. <u>aced</u>, m<u>eans</u>, d<u>id</u>, ex<u>tremely</u>, w<u>ell</u>
4. scr<u>ew</u>, t<u>est</u>, l<u>ab</u>, pr<u>oject</u>, m<u>eans</u>, r<u>uin</u>, d<u>o</u>, wr<u>ong</u>, w<u>ell</u>
5. C<u>ool</u>, v<u>ogue</u>, l<u>ong</u>, t<u>ime</u>, de<u>scribes</u>, th<u>ings</u>, f<u>un</u>, int<u>eresting</u>, gr<u>eat</u>
6. r<u>iot</u>, m<u>eans</u>, l<u>ot</u>, f<u>un</u>, co<u>mic</u>
7. str<u>essed</u>, up<u>set</u>, t<u>ense</u>
8. b<u>ummed</u>, de<u>pressed</u>, disap<u>pointed</u>
9. ps<u>yched</u>, f<u>eel</u>, ex<u>cited</u>, w<u>ell</u>, prep<u>ared</u>
10. w<u>asted</u>, dr<u>unk</u>, t<u>ired</u>
11. j<u>erk</u>, per<u>son</u>, be<u>haves</u>, an<u>noyingly</u>
12. j<u>ock</u>, a<u>thlete</u>, J<u>ocks</u>, h<u>ave</u>, i<u>mage</u>, sm<u>art</u>

W-5A. Final Key Rule Endings -ion, -iate, -ial, *etc.*

Exercise 1

1. bacter(ia, KSR
2. patr(iot, KSR
3. ~~steroids~~
4. experient(ial, KSR
5. ~~lion~~
6. immed(iately, KSR
7. ~~rioting~~
8. pat(iently, KSR
9. ~~terrain~~
10. gen(iuses, KSR
11. ment(ioned, KSR
12. anc(ient, KSR
13. ~~defied~~
14. ~~arteries~~
15. apprec(iating, KSR
16. ~~contaminate~~
17. ~~triumphs~~
18. dev(iantly, KSR
19. sal(ience, KSR
20. ~~pliant~~
21. ~~surliest~~
22. fallac(iously, KSR
23. ~~chandelier~~
24. ~~phial~~
25. consort(ium, KSR
26. ~~deceived~~

Exercise 2

1. guár̲d(ians
2. ambít̲(ious
3. expéd̲(iently
4. séct̲(ioning
5. aúd̲(iences
6. admíss̲(ion
7. pronunciát̲(ion
8. influént̲(ial
9. quót̲(ients
10. bríll̲(iantly
11. ideát̲(ion
12. epineúr̲(ium
13. fruít̲(ion
14. acquisít̲(ion
15. aúct̲(ioned
16. obséqu̲(iously
17. Háít̲(ian's
18. sén̲(ior
19. excrúc̲(iating
20. petít̲(ioned
21. maturát̲(ion
22. delineát̲(ion
23. ultér̲(ior
24. a dév̲(iance
25. inít̲(ially
26. nauseát̲(ion
27. collóqu̲(ial
28. initiát̲(ion
29. insoúc̲(iant
30. einstéín̲(ium
31. méd̲(iating
32. párt̲(ially
33. vacát̲(ioned
34. olýmp̲(iads

Exercise 3

Sit. 1: collóquium; ánxious, Geórgia; Indústrial, Revolútion
Sit. 2: psychosócial; Wílliams; brílliant, physícian
Sit. 3: communicátion; Bulgária; expérience; fináncially
Sit. 4: equátion; observátion, caútious
Sit. 5: quéstions, únion; negótiator, informátion

Exercise 4

1. exemplificátion, KSR
2. exémplifying, LSR
3. compánion, KSR
4. cómpany, LSR
5. résidency, VSR
6. residéntial, KSR
7. rádiator, KSR
8. radiátion, KSR
9. éstuary, PSR
10. estuárial, KSR
11. Órient, KSR
12. oriéntal, VSR
13. orientátion, KSR
14. auditórium, KSR
15. audítion, KSR
16. aúditory, PSR
17. áviator, KSR
18. aviátion, KSR
19. fámily, LSR
20. famílial, KSR
21. famíliar, KSR
22. objéction, KSR
23. objéctify, LSR
24. objéctive, PSR

W-5B. Nonfinal Key Rule Endings -ional, -iary, *etc.*

Exercise 1

1. intersect(ional, -al
2. X
3. commiss(ioner, -er
4. assoc(iative, -ive
5. unquest(ionable, -able
6. X
7. constitut(ional, -al
8. X
9. combinat(ional, -al
10. pass(ionate, -ate
11. quest(ioner, -er
12. X
13. X
14. requisit(ioner, -er
15. X
16. unment(ionable, -able

Exercise 2

1. congregat(ional
2. condit(ioner
3. situat(ional
4. deter(iorate
5. init(iative
6. act(ionable
7. dysfunct(ional
8. parish(ioner
9. unquest(ionable
10. ideat(ional
11. alleviate
12. init(ialer

Exercise 3

1. practít(ioner
2. compán(ionable
3. ideát(ional
4. unappréc(iative
5. amél(iorate
6. inít(iative
7. quést(ionable
8. vacát(ioner
9. compáss(ionate
10. situát(ional
11. petít(ioner
12. occás(ional
13. impréss(ionable
14. tradít(ional
15. rád(iative
16. uncónsc(ionable
17. assóc(iative
18. propórt(ionate

Exercise 4

1. institút(ionalize, -alize
2. creát(ionism, -ism
3. X
4. judíc(ialize, -ize
5. X
6. bríll(iancy, -y
7. retál(iatory, -ory
8. rát(ionalist, -alist
9. subsíd(iary, -y
10. rég(ionalism, -alism
11. memór(ialize, -ize
12. nutrít(ionist, -ist
13. stát(ionary, -ary
14. X
15. editór(ialize, -ize
16. X
17. extórt(ionist, -ist
18. conversát(ionalist, -alist
19. X
20. divérs(ionary, -ary
21. spéc(ialist, -ist
22. renúnc(iatory,-ory
23. X
24. X
25. intervént(ionism, -ism
26. reconcíl(iatory, -ory
27. sensát(ionalism, -alism
28. rég(ionalize, -alize

Exercise 5

1. trívialize
2. conversátional
3. detériorate
4. éxpiatory
5. váriative
6. evolútionist
7. ídiocy
8. fúnctionalism
9. internát(ionalize
10. cáutioner
11. sensátional
12. recéss(ionary
13. objéctionable
14. abstráct(ionism
15. proféss(ionalize
16. Confúc(ianism
17. áct(ionable
18. auxíl(iary
19. nát(ionalist
20. parliamentár(ianism
21. díct(ionary

Exercise 6

1. vísionary, KSR
2. vísual, VSR
3. ségregated, LSR
4. segregátionist, KSR
5. illúsionary, KSR
6. illúsory, PSR
7. reconciliátion, KSR
8. reconcíliatory, KSR
9. cóngregate, LSR
10. Congregátionalist, KSR
11. variabílity, LSR
12. váriative, KSR
13. obsérvatory, PSR
14. observátional, KSR
15. benévolent, VSR
16. benefíciary, KSR
17. expréssionism, KSR
18. expréssive, PSR
19. mémory, PSR
20. memórialize, KSR
21. memorizátion, KSR
22. práctical, VSR
23. practicálity, LSR
24. practítioner, KSR

W-6A. V/VC Rule Endings -al, -ous, ic

Exercise 1

1. patriarch(al, VSR
2. ~~proposal~~
3. ~~insidious~~
4. adventur(ous, VSR
5. ~~alluvial~~
6. orient(al, VSR
7. liter(al, VSR
8. atypic(al, VSR
9. ambigu(ous, VSR
10. ~~renewal~~
11. nocturn(al, VSR
12. ~~obvious~~
13. humor(ous, VSR
14. ~~refusal~~

Exercise 2

1. mystic(al
2. neutr(al
3. gratuit(ous
4. annu(al
5. procedur(al
6. moment(ous
7. circuit(ous
8. clinic(al
9. vir(al
10. nebul(ous
11. acoustic(al
12. contemptu(ous

Exercise 3

1. volúmin(ous, L
2. dígit(ally, L
3. overzeal(ous, K
4. maníac(al, L
5. cuboíd(al, K
6. hypothétic(ally, L
7. stupénd(ous, K
8. rádic(al, L
9. fáctu(al, L
10. conspícu(ous, L
11. prósper(ous, L
12. semiánnu(al, L
13. bilíngu(al, K
14. disloý(al, K
15. periodónt(al, K
16. náutic(al, L
17. úsu(al, L
18. periódic(ally, L
19. supplemént(al, K
20. ancéstr(al, K

Exercise 4

1. inorgánic, L
2. ubíquitous, L
3. electrónics, L
4. biánnually, L
5. intrínsic, L
6. continéntal, K
7. miráculous, L
8. crítical, L
9. enthusiástic, L
10. strénuously, L
11. mosáic, L
12. aeronáutical, L
13. enórmously, K
14. myópic, L
15. rígorous, L
16. Mesozóic, L
17. dángerous, L
18. developméntal, K

Exercise 5

1. instruméntal, VSR
2. instrumentátion, KSR
3. mathemátics, VSR
4. mathematícian, KSR
5. morphólogy, LSR
6. amórphous, VSR
7. hallucinogénic, VSR
8. hallúcinatory, PSR
9. hallinátion, KSR
10. technológical, VSR
11. technícian, KSR
12. téchnical, VSR

13. technólogy, LSR
14. anónymous, VSR
15. anonýmity, LSR
16. neútral, VSR
17. neutrálity, LSR
18. prospérity, LSR
19. prósperous, VSR
20. órdinary, PSR
21. órdinal, VSR
22. ordinátion, KSR
23. stúpefy, LSR
24. stupéndous, VSR

W-6B. V/VC Rule Endings -Vnt, -Vnce, -Vncy

Exercise 1

1. particip(ants, VSR
2. delinqu(ency, VSR
3. ~~implant~~
4. issu(ance, VSR
5. ~~expediency~~
6. ~~discontented~~
7. occup(ancy, VSR
8. tru(ants, VSR
9. frequ(ency, VSR

10. ~~luxuriant~~
11. differ(ent, VSR
12. repent(ant, VSR
13. ~~repenting~~
14. pres(ence, VSR
15. acquaint(ance, VSR
16. ~~ingredients~~
17. ~~advocacy~~
18. reminisc(ent, VSR

Exercise 2

1. préfer(ences, L
2. órdin(ance, L
3. annóy(ances, K
4. redúnd(ancy, K
5. cóyen(ant, L
6. fréqu(ent, K
7. présid(ent, L
8. flambóy(ant, K
9. adolésc(ent, K
10. constítu(ency, L
11. perpétu(ance, L
12. bál(ance, K
13. expéct(antly, K

14. ámbul(ance, L
15. resúlt(ant, K
16. extrávag(ancies, L
17. predícam(ent, L
18. flúctu(ant, L
19. perfórm(ance, K
20. irrélev(ancy, L
21. víol(ent, L
22. revérber(ant, L
23. frágr(antly, K
24. cómplim(ent, L
25. áccid(ent, L
26. consúlt(ancy, K

Exercise 3

1. íncident, VSR
2. incidéntal, VSR
3. lubrícious, KSR
4. lúbricant, VSR
5. lubrícity, LSR
6. týranny, LSR
7. týrant, VSR
8. tyránnical, VSR
9. admíttance, VSR
10. admíssive, PSR
11. admíssion, KSR
12. residéntial, KSR
13. résident, VSR
14. resídual, VSR
15. cógnitive, PSR
16. cognítion, KSR
17. cógnizant, VSR
18. víolated, LSR
19. violátion, KSR
20. víolent, VSR
21. partícipant, VSR
22. partícipatory, PSR
23. sacrilégious, KSR
24. sácrament, VSR

W-7A. Left Rule Endings -y/-i on Long Words

Exercise 1

1. strateg(y, LSR
2. ~~dolly~~
3. edif(y, LSR
4. ~~allegory~~
5. ~~booty~~
6. hypocris(y, LSR
7. typif(ies, LSR
8. apostas(y, LSR
9. histolog(y, LSR
10. ~~consistency~~
11. ~~periphery~~
12. signif(y, LSR
13. ~~ferry~~
14. symphon(ies, LSR
15. ~~occupancy~~
16. ~~luminary~~
17. proximit(y, LSR
18. ~~implies~~
19. anxiet(ies, LSR
20. classif(ier, LSR

Exercise 2

1. strateg(y
2. courtes(y
3. edif(y
4. cruelt(y
5. cardiolog(y
6. commonalit(ies
7. classifi(er
8. heterogeneit(y
9. philosoph(y
10. perpetuit(y
11. signif(y
12. hegemon(y

Exercise 3

1. fórtif(ied
2. líturg(ies
3. cólon(y
4. móllif(y
5. cómpan(y
6. courtes(y
7. éuphon(y
8. céntur(ies
9. biógraph(y
10. rívalr(ies
11. eléctrif(ying
12. spécif(ies
13. satíet(y
14. crúcif(ied
15. déit(y
16. clárif(y

Exercise 4
1. Análogies, vívify, clárify
2. Reliabílity, valídity, methodólogy
3. univérsities, strátegies, divérsity, ethnícity
4. publícity, abílity, fáculty
5. taxónomy, clássifies, abílity

Exercise 5

1. strátegies, LSR
2. stratégic, VSR
3. déstinies, LSR
4. approximátion, KSR
5. próximal, VSR
6. proxímity, LSR
7. exémplary, PSR
8. exémplify, LSR
9. mystified, LSR
10. mystérious, KSR
11. mystery's, LSR
12. hypocrítical, VSR
13. hypócrisy, LSR
14. herédity, LSR
15. heréditary, PSR
16. destinátion, KSR
17. admónitory, PSR
18. admonítions, KSR
19. unanímity, LSR
20. unánimous, VSR
21. índustry's, LSR
22. indústrious, KSR
23. sýmmetry, LSR
24. symmétrically, VSR

W-7B. Left Rule Endings -ate, -acy

Exercise 1
1. estimate, estimated, estimating, estimator
2. generate, generated, generating, generator
3. instigate, instigated, instigating, instigator
4. perpetrate, perpetrated, perpetrating, perpetrator

Exercise 2

1. calibr(ating, LSR
2. ~~belated~~
3. obstin(acy, LSR
4. ~~locate~~
5. ~~intermediate~~
6. dissemin(ated, LSR
7. privac(y, LSR
8. ~~berating~~
9. inaccur(acies, LSR
10. ~~excruciating~~
11. ~~restate~~
12. calcul(ator, LSR

Exercise 3

1. éxpurgate
2. accómmodating
3. éfficacy
4. intímidated
5. detérminacy
6. colláborated
7. íntimacies
8. degéneracy
9. incríminating
10. óbstinate
11. cándidacy
12. círculator
13. fúmigating
14. illúminated
15. conféderacy
16. enúmerated
17. démonstrator
18. incínerated

Exercise 4

undebáted, unsedáted, uninfláted, unreláted, interreláted, overinfláte, overráte, overstáte, overáte, underráte, understáte

Exercise 5

1. illúminate, LSR
2. lúminous, VSR
3. lúnacy, LSR
4. lúminary, PSR
5. repúdiated, KSR
6. appróximated, LSR
7. próximal, VSR
8. proxímity, LSR
9. celebrátion, KSR
10. célebrated, LSR
11. prelíminary, PSR
12. prélacy, LSR
13. ádvocacy, LSR
14. ádvocating, LSR
15. advísory, PSR
16. délegacy, LSR
17. delegátion, KSR
18. délegated, LSR
19. génerate, LSR
20. genéric, VSR
21. generátional, KSR
22. génerous, VSR
23. célibacy, LSR
24. delíciously, KSR
25. délicacies, LSR
26. illúsory, PSR
27. illústrious, KSR
28. íllustrator, LSR

W-8A. Prefixes and Stress

Exercise 1

1. ~~over~~apprehénsive
2. ~~super~~vísory
3. nonc
4. none
5. ~~contra~~indícative
6. none
7. ~~intro~~dúctory
8. ~~extra~~órdinary
9. none
10. ~~counter~~intúitive
11. ~~inter~~céssory
12. none
13. ~~retro~~spéctive
14. none

Exercise 2

1. prohíbitive, none
2. refútatory, re-
3. ~~super~~vísory, none
4. reprodúctive, pro-
5. reíterative, none
6. ~~over~~apprehénsive, pre-
7. ~~retro~~gréssive, none
8. prímitive, none
9. perfúnctory, per-
10. ~~over~~defénsive, de-
11. depósitory, none
12. unrespónsive, re-

Exercise 3

1. advísory, ad-
2. inóperative, none
3. subcúrative, sub-
4. ámbulatory, none
5. obsérvatory, ob-
6. ~~super~~abrásive, ab-
7. nonadhésive, ad-
8. sublíterature, none
9. apóthecary, none
10. ~~over~~obséssive, ob-
11. subvérsive, sub-
12. súmptuary, none

Exercise 4

1. intrúsive, in-
2. ~~inter~~céssory, none
3. compúlsory, com-
4. dýsentery, none
5. exémplary, ex-
6. infínitive, none

7. dispénsary, dis-
8. condúcive, con-
9. ~~extra~~órdinary, none
10. ~~over~~inclúsive, in-
11. discóvery, dis-
12. ~~contra~~díctory, none

Exercise 5

1. attráctive, at-
2. órdinary, none
3. effróntery, ef-
4. unimpréssive, im-
5. imáginary, none
6. applícative, ap-
7. diffúsive, dif-

8. elíminatory, none
9. offénsive, of-
10. áctuary, none
11. corrósive, cor-
12. allíterative, none
13. accéssory, ac-
14. cáricature, none

Exercise 6

1. illúsory, il-
2. nonadhésive, ad-
3. dispénsary, dis-
4. succéssive, suc-
5. státutory, none
6. ~~retro~~áctive, none
7. submíssive, sub-
8. ~~super~~indúctive, in-
9. collúsive, col-
10. incítory, in-
11. assúmptive, as-
12. ~~inter~~jéctory, none
13. affírmative, af-
14. invéstigatory, none
15. oppréssive, op-
16. ámbulatory, none
17. compúlsive, com-
18. provócative, pro-

19. itínerary, none
20. abstráctive, ab-
21. oblígatory, ob-
22. persónative, per-
23. consúmptive, con-
24. illúminative, none
25. allúsive, al-
26. propúlsive, pro-
27. ~~counter~~sígnature, none
28. expíratory, ex-
29. occlúsive, oc-
30. ~~over~~protéctive, pro-
31. ~~extra~~sénsory, none
32. refínery, re-
33. indecísive, de-
34. ~~super~~vísory, none
35. aggréssive, ag-
36. córollary, none

W-8B. Prefix Rule Endings -ary, -ery, -ory, -ive

Exercise 1

1. exempl(ary, PSR
2. ~~idolatry~~
3. categ(ories, PSR
4. ~~subsidiary~~
5. transit(ive, PSR
6. periph(eries, PSR
7. subvers(ive, PSR

8. ~~tertiary~~
9. exposit(ory, PSR
10. forg(ery, PSR
11. ~~economize~~
12. ~~weaponries~~
13. mis(ery, PSR
14. ~~discretionary~~

Exercise 2

1. in**fírm**(ary, K
2. **sávag**(ery, L
3. **víct**(ories, K
4. in**efféct**(ive, K
5. **púnit**(ory, L
6. in**quísit**(ively, L
7. **árt**(ery, K
8. over**illús**(ory, K

9. **mís**(ery, K
10. di**mínut**(ive, L
11. e**ffrónt**(ery, K
12. **émiss**(ary, L
13. com**púls**(ory, K
14. **únit**(ary, L
15. retro**áct**(ive, K
16. **sécond**(ary, L

Exercise 3

1. **tríbut**ary, L
2. com**pétit**ive, L
3. **nécess**arily or ne**céss**árily
4. di**stíll**eries, K
5. compli**mént**ary, K
6. **cháncell**ery, L
7. extra**órdin**arily or extraor**dín**árily
8. supple**mént**ary, K
9. **tránsit**ive, L
10. re**fráct**ory, K

11. **cómment**ary, L
12. **cémet**eries, L
13. **abús**ively, K
14. **sémin**ary, L
15. ex**téns**ively, K
16. **órdin**ary, L
17. super**vís**ory, K
18. **témpor**arily or tem**por**árily
19. **fórg**ery, K
20. contra**cépt**ive, K

Exercise 4

1. **nót**aries, PSR
2. noto**ríet**y, LSR
3. notifi**cát**ion, KSR
4. mo**mént**ous, VSR
5. **móment**ary, PSR
6. de**fínit**ive, PSR
7. defi**nít**ion, KSR
8. **dígnit**ary, PSR
9. **dígnif**ied, LSR
10. **lúmin**ous, VSR

11. **lúmin**ary, PSR
12. **sécret**ary, PSR
13. secre**tár**ial, KSR
14. in**fínit**y, LSR
15. in**fínit**ive, PSR
16. **líbr**aries, PSR
17. li**brár**ian, KSR
18. arbi**trát**ion, KSR
19. **árbit**rator, LSR
20. **árbit**rary, PSR

W-8C. Prefix Rule Endings -ative, -atory, -ature

Exercise 1

1. ~~miniature~~
2. legisl(ature, PSR
3. ~~appreciative~~
4. gener(ative, PSR
5. reform(atory, PSR
6. territ(ory, PSR

7. alliter(ative, PSR
8. ~~retaliatory~~
9. curv(ature, PSR
10. posit(ive, PSR
11. inflamm(atory, PSR
12. ~~conciliatory~~

Exercise 2
1. géner(ative, L
2. procrástin(atory, L
3. ór(atory, K
4. deróg(atory, K
5. alimént(ative, K
6. múscul(ature, L
7. indíc(ative, K
8. exclám(atory, K
9. hallúcin(atory, L

10. víbr(atory, K
11. provóc(ative, K
12. cáric(ature, L
13. inóper(ative, L
14. provís(atory, K
15. prél(ature, K
16. consérv(atory, K
17. spécul(ative, L
18. admínistr(ative, L

Exercise 3
1. législature, PSR
2. legálity, LSR
3. appéllative, PSR
4. appellátion, KSR
5. témperature, PSR
6. témperate, LSR
7. témporal, VSR
8. témporary, PSR
9. váriative, KSR
10. variabílity, LSR

11. várious, KSR
12. ímagery, PSR
13. imáginative, PSR
14. genéric, VSR
15. génerative, PSR
16. generálity, LSR
17. argumentátion, KSR
18. arguméntative, PSR
19. indícative, PSR
20. indicátion, KSR